beco

SHE WAS

A MEMOIR

SHELLEY BROUWER

outskirts
press

Outskirts Press, Inc.
http://www.outskirtspress.com

ISBN: 978-1-9772-0803-3

Outskirts Press and the "OP" logo are trademarks belonging to Outskirts Press, Inc.

PRINTED IN THE UNITED STATES OF AMERICA

To Jessie, and to Jason and to Curt, who knew her best,
loved her best, and didn't make a big deal out of it.

Table of Contents

Foreword

OF THE THREE of us, our sister was the youngest. She called us her siblings, and we adored her. Some days, most days really, this thing happens inside us, where it's hard to believe she actually died. She was a tremendous part of our lives and her leaving this earth hasn't changed that, even five years later.

Our sister was special. She was unapologetically herself; outgoing, funny, had the sweetest heart, and was perfectly unaffected by the everyday nonsense that the rest of us get bogged down with.

Our sister taught us patience and tolerance and about real, true love in ways that are immeasurable. The limits to her physical and mental abilities somehow created in her a limitless optimism where love for others and trust in herself knew no bounds. Growing up, we taught her to adapt to our world but really all along she was refining us to be more like her. She taught us to love without judgement and about unfaltering hope in the face of pain and fear. Because of who she was, we've become who we are.

Our sister was brave and strong. At an early age, she learned how to face her challenges head-on. She got that strength and bravery from our mom. Our mom taught us all how to overcome obstacles and break through barriers most moms would have a hard time navigating. She selflessly protected our child-hearts and worked hard to keep our lives normal, while ensuring we knew how special we all were.

Our mom says that raising our sister was the greatest honor of her life. We understand that because the greatest honor of ours, was having the little sister we did. This story is a reflection of our mom's life and the things she learned from our sister along the way. We are so proud of our mom for all she's done, and we're proud that she's sharing it with all of you. We can't wait for you to read this book and hope that when you do, these stories will give you a taste of what we've been lucky enough to feel.

Jessie and Jason
(The Siblings)

In Japan, broken objects are often repaired with gold. Flaws and breaks are embraced and seen as something unique and beautiful.

1

Twenty-Two Years, Nine Months, Fifteen Days Old

THE ONLY THING our girl ever did completely on her own, without me, without my help or assistance in one way or another, was die.

I received a call from the assisted living home we'd moved her into only a few days earlier, telling me to, "Come quick, we can't get a pulse."

She died on a Thursday morning without a familiar face by her side. No family member; no one she knew well. She was twenty-two years, nine months and fifteen days old. She died at 7:30 am.

I arrived at 7:50.

The lovely woman who ran the house met me in the entryway where she took hold of both my arms and looked me squarely in the eyes. She didn't utter a sound. When I stammered the only words I could muster, "Is she........?", she nodded her head very slightly, then guided me down the hall, to the last door on the left where she stood back with other staff members to allow me to enter on my own.

I remember rushing to place my hand on the round antique-brass door handle, in my need to see and touch and be next to my youngest born child, then hesitating just for a second, wondering if I actually had to open the door— knowing that once I did life would be forever changed.

I stepped into her bright, cheery room that seemed dressed completely wrong for the occasion, with its white eyelet curtains catching the morning light and its vase of bright red flowers sitting on the desk. I found her tucked into bed looking peaceful and asleep. The turquoise blanket, the one with her name embroidered on it that her Aunt Kelly had given her for Christmas just a few months before, was pulled up - neck high.

She died twenty minutes earlier, and twenty minutes before that she was dressed and bright-eyed sitting at the breakfast table in her wheelchair with the rest of the residents eating breakfast.

And then, she choked on her pancakes.

The choice I made that day – to meet a friend for an early breakfast instead of going straight to the assisted living house — is a choice that taunts me with what-ifs and whys and should-haves and could-haves.

Why did I go to breakfast? (I don't even like breakfast.)

Why didn't I just go straight to the house?

Would she have died had I been there?

Could I have saved her? Should I have saved her? Or was

it time to let her go?

Was she scared? (Oh, how I pray she wasn't.)

Would I have been able to comfort her?

Would she even have known I was there?

Would my being there have mattered?

Did she see "the light"?

Were angels with her?

Was my mom with her?

Was God with her?

(Oh, how I pray that she wasn't alone.)

Did she know what was happening? Would I have known?

What did I miss?

Was she relieved?

Was she scared? (That one hurts the most.)

Was she joyful? Was she calm? Would I have been able to tell?

Would it have been better for her had I been there, or would my being there have made dying harder?

Maybe my presence (there or not) was of no significance.

Maybe it was though…. maybe we both needed me *not* to be there. Maybe that was the grand plan, and maybe that was what was best for her, and maybe that was what was best for me.

Without me, all on her own, she accepted the invitation to a better life. Maybe her last act of placing her big old hand into the even bigger, stronger hand held out to her, was her way of telling me, "It's okay Mom, we've got this from here, I'm going to be okay."

This, on good days, which are most days, is what I believe to be true. On the bad days though, those days that continue to come now and again, (the days that try as I might, I can think of nothing else) I can hardly bear the thought that I wasn't there when she needed me most.

It's those days that I wonder if she called my name.

2

One Month Old

I GAVE BIRTH to a baby girl in 1991 who wasn't perfect. Perfect like all babies are supposed to be. Perfect, like beauty, though, is seen through the eye of the beholder, isn't it? To me, she was perfect. All nine pounds and three ounces of her.

Her head was especially large, and not very round. Her head seemed almost square, and to top it off, she had something my irreverent brother refers to as a fivehead — a forehead that was unusually large.

Instead of the rosy pink skin her brother and sister had been born with, hers had a ruddy red tone to it, making it look like her entire body, from head to toe, had been scrubbed vigorously with a coarse cloth.

She had an umbilical hernia, which in her case meant her belly button ballooned out… a lot. Hers was the size of one of those big marbles, the ones we used to call Shooters, or better yet, the same size as a giant Jawbreaker that comes from a quarter gumball machine.

It seemed like God wanted her debut from the womb to be especially impressive. She arrived in this world with what appeared to be a light coating of red lipstick on her lips, perfectly applied, except for the top right where it looked like a pre-schooler had gotten to it. The coloring had run off her lips and onto the skin between her upper lip and nose. Later we found out the layman term for this type of birthmark was port-wine stain. I'd seen them before on people's faces or heads (Mikhail Gorbachev's for example) and wondered about them. I preferred the term a hospital nurse used to describe it: she called it the kiss of an angel.

My perfect baby had these tiny little flaps of extra skin, one on the side of her left pinky finger near the bottom where it attached to her hand, and the other at the base of her tailbone. They were as small as one little sprinkle atop a cupcake, but on her very light, smooth skin they stood out. Nurses told us these could be easily removed.

Her alert eyes were dark like mine, and bright, but also prominent and kind of bulgy.

None of this was obvious to me when they placed her in my arms just after her birth. I took stock of the fact that she had all the right parts, and they were all in the right places. She had two arms, two legs, two ears, two eyes, ten fingers, and ten toes. She cried and was breathing. I was enamored with her head full of dark curls and her fat little face. I saw her through the eyes of a mother, and I loved what I saw.

It would be days before I began to recognize that she had abnormalities. And a few days more before I knew that those abnormalities indicated to doctors the need to take a closer look at my perfect new child. It would be weeks before my good friend Laurie (a neonatal nurse) sat me down at my kitchen table and bravely told me that she had concerns about my perfect new baby's muscle tone. And it would be months before I saw these issues evolve into developmental delays - (no reaching for toys, no rolling over), and health issues - (recurring respiratory and spinal fluid infections).

I saw my sweet new baby through rose-colored glasses, as, I suppose, all mothers do. I wanted my baby to be perfect. My baby was perfect, except she wasn't. She was different, she was unique, and by the grace of God those facts were being revealed to me slowly, just a few at a time, until I somehow gained the courage to remove the rose-colored glasses.

Without the glasses I gave my baby the gift of seeing her as she truly was, and began to love this sweet child of mine as I was supposed to. In order to help her make her way in this world, I'd need to see her clearly. In order to help my little family through the challenges we were sure to face, it was imperative I see her clearly.

Sometimes my twenty-twenty vision hurt and made me want to close my eyes. More often though, it verified what my heart knew to be true, that perfect, like beauty, is in the eye of the beholder.

3

Three Months Old

THE FIRST FEW months after the birth of our youngest daughter, we had more questions than answers. While we waited in limbo for doctors and therapists to come up with the diagnosis that best fit our new baby's unusual physical characteristics (characteristics the doctors referred to as anomalies) we were unsure and almost unable to move forward. Because her symptoms didn't fall in line with any known disease or well-known syndrome, an obvious diagnosis was elusive, and the answers we looked for surrounding her general health and development were not apparent. Our pediatrician had us running from specialist to specialist in an attempt to rule out or confirm various possibilities. Much had been ruled out, very little confirmed. The answers we desperately needed regarding what to expect were nonexistent. We tried to stay positive; we tried to be patient.

While we waited, we play acted at life.

Whenever I found myself needing a short break from reality, I'd head to the small brick porch off the front of our house. That porch was a place of refuge for me and was the farthest place I'd allow myself to wander from the three small people back in the house who counted on me.

My front porch was comfortable. My vantage point on the cozy red rocking chair tucked behind the tall brick pillar allowed me to view the world going on around me without having to take part in that world or to be seen by it. I watched as kids in our neighborhood rode by on colorful bikes and noisy in-line skates. I watched as families dragged old-school American Flyer wagons laden with towels and kids and toys up to the swimming pool. I watched with a self-pitying and envious eye as my neighbors drove in and out. From my spot on the front porch, I watched my eager neighbors receive deliveries and packages that they couldn't wait to open. We received quite a few deliveries and packages those days too, though ours weren't so exciting. The deliveries we received were of oxygen tanks, medicines, and breathing machines.

That front porch was a safe place for me, and I escaped to it almost every afternoon. That front porch was the perfect location for my daily pity parties.

One warm fall day, as I hid out behind the pillar waiting for my party to begin, the loud ring of the clunky cordless phone that I brought with me everywhere (for fear that I'd miss a call from a doctor or a lab) yanked me back to reality. Answering the phone, I heard the comforting voice of a doctor I knew well. This doctor wasn't calling with test results or with news of my baby; this doctor was calling only to check on me. I was happy for his call. This was the doctor that had delivered my last two babies. He was one of the good guys, one of the doctors who listened to me and truly heard what I had to say. He was a man I considered an advisor and a friend. I remember telling him that day that I wished I possessed a crystal ball to show me the future. Not the forever future, just five years down the road future. I thought five years would surely give me enough to work with. I thought with five years' knowledge I'd be able to plan accordingly with answers to questions like:

Will she walk?

Will she communicate?

How will she communicate?

Will she be healthy?

Will she go to school?

Will she have friends?

Will we have to move or remodel our house to accommodate her needs?

What effect will all of this have on my other children?

What effect will all of this have on my marriage?

I also remember telling my doctor-friend-advisor that I thought I would rather have a physically challenged child than a child with deficient cognitive capacities. I remember thinking that it would pain me more not to be able to share an intelligent conversation with my daughter than to physically carry her. He listened, he dug a little deeper, he got me to elaborate, and he got me to think. He didn't offer an opinion, nor did he try to guide the direction of the conversation. He didn't try to appease me. He listened, without trying to make me feel better. And I just talked, without trying to make him feel better, which is what I caught myself doing when I spoke with others about my child and her undiagnosed disabilities; somehow I thought it my responsibility to offer them assurance. Our phone call ended. Time had come for me to get back inside the house. The pity party for the day was over.

Later that day, folding laundry into three distinct stacks: two-year-old Jason's Ninja Turtle underwear, six-year-old Jessie's pink dance leotards, and the baby's white Onesies, I questioned myself on the words I'd spoken earlier, the words that sounded like a bad game of Would You Rather. I thought about what I said - that I would rather have a child with physical disabilities than a child with cognitive disabilities, then right on cue, was hit with a memory from when I was ten years old. I was in the fourth grade, and the teacher was telling us what an important day it was for us. She told us that a group of kids with disabilities who attended a "special" school were being brought to hang out with us just for the day. She told us that we'd get to play with them and show them what it was like to go to our school. This was the '60s - that's how things were done back then.

My friends and I played out on the elementary school's hot gravel yard. A few of us were playing with a round-faced, blonde-haired, blue-eyed boy who wore an enormous and ceaseless grin. We played with him on the swings, and I remember being awed by the strength of his legs and how high he was able to get himself in the air. We rode with him on the Merry-Go-Round, laughing and holding on to each other for support. When we were done playing, he stood with us in a circle and talked. We had the best time with this boy who seemed to be having the best time with us. This boy with the huge grin, who ran a little slower than we did and spoke a little differently too, charmed us. It wasn't until later that I learned this boy had something called Down's Syndrome.

I don't remember that boy's name, and I have no idea what happened to him because I never saw him again. He went back to his school, and I continued on at mine. This was the '60's - that's how things were done back then.

How grateful I was, twenty years later, to be reminded of the boy and the quick connection we'd made. The little inclusion experiment, short-lived as it was, stuck with me. Thank you, teachers from the '60s, thank you boy from the fourth grade,..... I wonder where those strong legs of yours ended up taking you?

It occurred to me then, standing in the laundry room, folding my own kids' clothes, that I didn't know anyone with a significant disability, and it occurred to me then that my Would-You-Rather answer was selfishly and ignorantly based on what I thought would be easiest and most comfortable........ for me.

That's the day my thinking began to evolve, and the day that I began to stop concentrating on what I thought would be best for my daughter (which had a lot to do with what would be best for me), and focus instead on helping this girl, with whatever abilities she'd been born, to see herself as nothing less than perfect. I'd be there as a guide not as a manipulator — I'd help her live the life she would choose to live, instead of the life I'd choose for her.

Learning to delight in just who my girl was, instead of who she wasn't, kind of put an end to the pity parties. They quickly became less sad, and therefore less effective in a pity party sort of way. Eventually, I mostly stopped feeling sorry for myself and got on again with the sweetness and busyness of living. The pity parties, well, at least the regularly scheduled ones, magically just faded away.

4

Three to Seven Months Old

THE WHIRLWIND WE lived in began to settle into just a dust storm by the time she was three months old. We were doing a pretty decent job of figuring out how to be parents to three kids instead of two, and were somehow coming up with the extra hours it took to schedule and attend all of the doctor appointments our new littlest one required, without disrupting, too much, the active, happy lives of our older two.

Then our pediatrician threw us a curve ball.

He told us if our baby was to thrive, we'd need to get her into physical, occupational and speech therapy as soon as possible. He also told us there was something called Early Intervention for "kids like ours" meaning kids who weren't reaching those important first milestones, and he told us that our girl wasn't. At two months she wasn't even close to holding her head up, and by four, although interested, didn't appear to be reaching for things held out for her. Early Intervention, he said was for kids who were developing slowly. He then admitted that he didn't know that much about Early Intervention and not so much about therapies either, but he knew there were classes, and he knew there were programs out there for "people like us." He maintained he thought it was important and also maintained, that we look into it, whatever "it" was, right away.

That well-meaning pediatrician, who we left a few months later when we found someone better suited to work with our family, wasn't connected to the world of disability. He was connected to the world of kids that were well, or would most likely get well. He knew how to take care of broken arms and how to medicate strep throat. Our kid had more than that, but at four months we were still waiting for a definitive diagnosis.

We weren't connected to the world of disability either, but we found ourselves thrown into the middle of it. We were in a foreign land, without a guide, and just beginning our journey. The medical terrain we were trudging through seemed challenging enough, and when we learned there was therapeutic ground we needed to cover with a language all its own, we felt we'd stepped onto a land-mine. The safe place we'd always lived, where kids were healthy and developed pretty much as they were supposed to, was gone. My husband Don and I were clueless on which way to go or what to do, and we were the ones in charge, the grown-ups - the parents. We needed to figure it out.

Knowing that our hours of research weren't getting us anywhere except tired and confused and that we had teams of medical professionals hot on the diagnosis pursuit, we took our pediatrician's advice about checking into therapy and Early Intervention. It was 1991, the World Wide Web wasn't really a thing then, and information was difficult to access. So what precious free time I had, while Jason napped, and Jess was at school for the day, I now spent on the phone, trying to figuring out exactly what types of programs and services were out there for "kids like ours", what programs and services she would be eligible for based upon her needs, and just what programs and services we'd be able to afford.

With just one phone call, I received a quick and painful education from our insurance company. I learned that, in their opinion, she'd be just fine. In fact, anyone with a disability of any type would be just fine with the eight magical visits per YEAR they would approve for physical therapy, along with the eight magical visits per YEAR they'd provide for occupational therapy, and if absolutely needed, they'd even throw in eight visits per YEAR for speech therapy. Anything more than that would be on us.

Early Intervention, it turns out, was merely a catch-all phrase for services intended to help infants and toddlers with disabilities and their families. Early Intervention Services could include nutrition assistance, speech, language and hearing tests, counseling services for the family, or physical and occupational therapy. Early Intervention Services were offered by private and government agencies, and by specific groups like The Down's Syndrome Association, or the Cerebral Palsy Support Organization, or the Autism Society, which we couldn't join since our girl had not been diagnosed with any of these conditions.

I called the agencies who offered Early Intervention Services and explained to them what we knew about our daughter.

I described her extremely low muscle tone, explaining that she was as floppy as a Raggedy Ann doll, but countered with how very alert she was, saying that her eyes didn't miss a thing. I told them how well she ate, and that doctors had concerns about the size of her huge seemingly square head and the fact that she didn't have the strength to hold it up on her own, but told them too, how beautiful the dark curls were that adorned it. I told them that the reddish or ruddy tone of her skin couldn't be explained and that doctors were looking for underlying problems or syndromes, but that conclusive results were still out. I explained how her eyes lit up when she looked at us and how our hearts melted when we held her. I explained to them that this was our girl, and that we adored her. And then I waited for help, or guidance or suggestions, which usually led to more phone calls and more explanations and some hope.

Navigating the system on our own, we looked to the phone book, which seemed sort of logical at the time, for a pediatric physical therapist. We found one who lived close by and worked out of her home. We checked her references (but honestly, what provider would give out names and numbers of clients who would give poor references?) and decided to go with her.

After dropping our oldest off at school and our middle child off at a friend's house, I stood holding my precious bundle in my arms and waited for the therapist to answer her door. She invited us into her home where she took the baby from me to get a better look. I watched, as I had watched many others over the last few months unwrap and examine my sweet girl. She did it methodically and systematically, explaining what she was doing and why. Oh, how I longed for people to ooh and ahh over my baby; instead they nodded, took notes, and used measuring tapes to record the anomalies they found. I watched as the therapist assessed my girl's muscle tone by moving her arms and legs up and down and in and out. I watched as she applied pressure to the bottoms of her feet to see if the baby would push back. I had to stop myself from jumping up as I watched the therapist, in an effort to determine neck strength, pull the baby up by her arms as she lay on her back—-without supporting her neck and head as I was always so careful to do.

The therapist and I had no emotional connection. I'm pretty sure there was no connection between her and her newest little client either. The therapist suggested that we return in a week, and in the meantime, showed me a few exercises that we were to work on at home twice a day, for about twenty minutes each time. The homework was supposed to improve strength and trigger muscle memory. The therapist gave me a few sheets of black and white illustrated handouts to remind me of the work we were to do. I made an appointment for the following week, wrapped my girl back up and left.

Over the next few days, I carved more time, that I didn't have, out of the day to follow through on the homework. I'd lay the baby on the floor, with the paperwork and diagrams close by and begin to manipulate her little arms and legs and torso, the way I was supposed to.

I was afraid.

I was nervous.

What if I hurt her?

I was clumsy.

I didn't know what I was doing.

Lay the baby prone.......

-what does that mean?

check the handout.

oh, face down.

…..across your lap…….

-which way, vertical or horizontal?

check the handout.

oh, horizontal.

Place your right hand under baby's bottom and your left hand under baby's left arm…….

- wait, which one is her left? she's laying on her tummy, so yeah, this one is her left,

….. Twist baby away from you into a sitting position…..

- huh?

check handout.

My hair would fall over my eyes, and my arms were always in the way. I didn't want to lose ground by brushing the hair out of my eyes, and I didn't want to readjust my arms for fear I'd lose ground already gained. Reading the instructions before beginning the exercises wasn't the answer either.

There was just too much to remember.

This was all too new- too different.

The therapist made it look easy.

It wasn't easy.

I stuck with it, twice a day every day.

And the baby stuck with it too: she was good.

She didn't seem to mind or notice my inadequacies.

We went back to the therapist every week, sometimes my mom came with us, and sometimes my husband Don. Each of them tried their hands at the homework too, and unfortunately, were no better at it than I was, which oddly enough, gave me a twisted sense of reassurance.

We continued on—— hoping, but not sure if we were making a difference.

My search for help, at last, led me to an agency that served children with disabilities in the city and county where we lived. I was delighted when I made an appointment with a woman who told me we didn't need to pack up and come to her, but that instead, she would come to us. She told me not to worry about getting a babysitter for the other kids, that she'd be happy to meet all of us at our house. She said that when we met she'd be able to explain the services her agency could offer our family.

The day of the meeting arrived. I didn't know whether to clean up the house so that it looked nice or mess it up a bit to make it look like we were in some real need. I couldn't decide if I should bake cookies and have coffee ready, or offer nothing. I defaulted, as is my way, to the cookies, coffee and cleaning bit, but then began to agonize over the fact that maybe I was making everything too nice. I began to imagine that the lady would think that I had some nerve, calling her to come to my brand new house where everything seemed perfectly under control—-oh, except for the one thing, the baby with all the issues. In my head, I was sure the woman would take one step in the door, grab a cookie and say she had other families who needed her more than we did. Before I had a chance to over-turn the couch, throw the cookies in the trash, and change into worn jeans with holes in the knees, the doorbell rang.

The woman who I greeted at the door with a big smile and warm handshake (trying to be as friendly as I could because I wanted her to like us, and because I wanted her to help us) was shy but kind, and far younger than I'd imagined. She seemed almost as uneasy as I was.

While the baby slept peacefully upstairs in her crib, the young woman and I sat down to cookies and coffee at the kitchen table. I asked her if she'd like to meet my daughter. I offered to wake her up or suggested that we could go upstairs just to take a peek. She declined both offers. We talked for a while. She wrote down the information I supplied her on her necessary government forms. She ate a cookie. She sipped on coffee. She brought me very little written information, but she told me her agency had baby groups facilitated by therapists who could give us suggestions for daily life with a child with a disability. She told me I would meet other mothers dealing with similar situations. She told me that there were groups for brothers and sisters. She told me they had resource suggestions. She told me there were funding opportunities. She told me that her agency had people who could offer us moral and emotional support. She told me that to access all of this my girl would need to be evaluated by a team of professionals. She told me how crucial Early Intervention was and how important it was to start it as soon as possible. She didn't look me in the eye when she told me the soonest appointment she had was 45 days away. She was efficient and businesslike. When I mentioned that we already had enough evaluations to fill a small library, she told me that if we were to use her agency (which was government funded) we had to go through their evaluation. I wanted what she had to offer. I made an appointment for the evaluation, and the young woman left. She never met my daughter.

Our daughter would be almost seven months old by the time the evaluation was complete, and the results we expected were in. She was developmentally delayed. She did qualify for services. And that's when I was told that there was a waiting list, and the wait would be well over a year. And that's when the mention of severe underfunding by the state and the federal government came up. And that's when we were offered the opportunity to participate in playgroups with other families on the waiting list.

And that's when I got back on the phone.

5

Three to Eight Months Old

THE FIRST TIME doctors informed us our youngest child's life was in danger, she was three months old. Until that day the only thing doctors had been certain of were that the ventricles in her brain (the fancy way of saying the cavities where spinal fluid is produced) were somewhat enlarged, and that it was possible for enlarged ventricles to lead to hydrocephalus (the fancy way of saying water-on-the-brain). Doctors were monitoring the situation closely with bi-weekly ultra sounds or CT scans to determine when or if her condition would require surgery. They referred to the surgery as shunt surgery and described how a piece of tubing would be threaded from her brain to her abdomen to redirect any excess fluid and relieve the building pressure on her brain, which all sounded scary enough—but doctors felt sure there was something more to our girl's anomalies than hydrocephalus.

Doctors assured us that if hydrocephalus actually did develop (meaning that her ventricles filled with more fluid than they could handle) hydrocephalus was a condition easily lived with. Hydrocephalus, doctors told us in her case at least - was not life threatening, and hydrocephalus, doctors told us, if treated early was *not* a certain cause of developmental delay. If hydrocephalus occurred, doctors were confident a shunt would provide relief.

While teams of doctors searched, we waited and tried, as best we could, to live our lives.

And then I received a call from our pediatrician that changed everything. He was calling to say that the metabolic doctors, the super smart docs who spent years studying biochemistry as well as medicine, had found something. He didn't say what, but said those doctors wanted to meet with us immediately in the Emergency Department at Children's Hospital.

My mom rushed over to watch the older kids.

I rushed from home with the baby.

Don rushed from work.

We were met by a team of research doctors in an overcrowded inner-city Emergency Room. Crying children and distraught parents were everywhere. Our doctors, explaining that their laboratory lacked suitable meeting space, ushered us into a small interior room without windows. There were six of us (including the baby I held in my arms) squashed into a space that couldn't have been much better than their laboratory and its unsuitable meeting space. The chairs that each of us sat on were the doctor rolling type of chair, better known as a stool. The room we were in wasn't a meeting room, or an exam room, a treatment room, or a work space. The room felt like what it was, an extra room that someone had just rolled some stools into.

Naively, I was actually excited. Naively, I was sure we were going to receive good news, news that would help us. In my heart of hearts, I believed we would be given medication and all of her symptoms would disappear.

That was not the news we received.

There would be no medication.

The doctors began to describe an extremely rare metabolic disorder that had something to do with the body's inability to break down amino acids.

They told us the defining characteristic of the disorder were muscle spasms, and that once the muscle spasms began they would never cease. Never.

They believed our girl had this disorder.

Doctors couldn't predict when the muscle spasms would begin ("could be a year, could be sooner"), but when they began, the count down on her life would begin as well. They couldn't predict how long she'd be able to live with the spasms, but they were talking months not years.

Her body would move or twist or twitch or bend, all the time, even when she slept—if sleep she'd be able. We were told that eventually her body would wear itself out from exhaustion.

The doctors stressed the rarity of the disorder and their frustration over the fact that there was very little data to share.

This though, they knew for sure: there was no cure.

The research doctors told us they were 98% certain of their diagnosis. One last lab result (a skin culture which needed to grow for another 60 days) would provide absolute confirmation. The doctors believed our best avenue of defense was to immediately begin work with a dietician/nutritionist who could help us, through supplements, add amino acids to our baby's diet (which consisted entirely of baby formula) that her little body might have a chance of breaking down.

As the doctors spoke, the tiny room we were in seemed to grow narrower and longer and excruciatingly more warm. The experience I had is difficult to describe. I heard the doctors, I could even respond to them, but remember feeling that I was an observer of the conversation instead of a participant. From a vantage point high up near the ceiling, in the far corner of the room, I watched the scene below me unfold.

I was detached, and at the same time present. I watched myself hold and rock the precious bundle my arms held. I took note of the anguish on my husband's face, and noticed the awkward and uncomfortable way one of the doctors held his hands, moving them from his lap to his sides, and then back again, like he didn't know what to do with them. I watched the other doctor's lips move and I watched myself function efficiently, performing I suppose, what I thought was expected:

take care of the baby

hold yourself together

ask rational questions

listen and remember what the doctors are saying

figure out how to handle this

don't cry too much

High up near the ceiling, in the corner of that little room, I was terrified and frozen.

Somehow, my body and my mind acted independently of each other.

I don't remember anything else about that meeting or that night except my drive home. Don took the baby and I drove myself since we had two cars. Alone, I let my guard down. Alone in my car, I cried, I screamed, I prayed, I begged, I cursed, and I hurt......

Alone in my car, I allowed myself to feel. Alone in my car, I began to grieve.

When people ask how we carried on once we had the knowledge of the ticking-time-bomb diagnosis, my answer is always the same: "We just did." "We had to." "What other choice was there?" We had three kids; two who needed to go to school and one who needed to go to doctor appointments. Each of them needed to be fed, and bathed, and played with. We loved each of them, and each of them deserved our attention. We carried on by doing normal everyday things: we went to the park, we went to the grocery store, we went to work. We watched movies, we filled the car with gas, we cleaned the house, we cried and we laughed and we continued to live and continued to wait.

My parents helped us tirelessly. They brought dinners, they babysat, they did the laundry and helped with household chores, they listened, they counseled and they put their lives on hold for us. Their ache ran deep — they too had a daughter whose ails they couldn't fix.

We tirelessly searched for more information and followed the nutritionist's guidelines for adding the supplements to our baby's diet that could help her. The supplements came only in capsule form so our routine, three times a day and best handled by two adults, went something like this:

break the capsules apart

hold her mouth open (at just the right angle)

pour the chalky orange powder into her mouth, then quickly........so she'll swallow—

shove the baby bottle in her mouth with a chaser of formula

After each feeding she'd be covered in orange, we'd be covered in orange, and we never knew how much of the stuff she actually ingested.

Nights and early mornings were the hardest. Don and I would get in bed and usually fall asleep talking about our fears. In the morning, while the house was still quiet, I'd sit in the old white rocking chair, in the corner of her bedroom between the two curtained windows, and feed her.

I had an infant, I was sleep deprived and had that foggy feeling that comes with the territory. I liked to keep the room dark so that neither one of us would get over stimulated early in the morning. I'd watch her eat through the dusky light trying to make its way through the windows, and imagine (each time she twitched her arm or moved her leg) that the movement-that-would-never-stop had begun. I'd hold my breath and feel my stomach lurch. I'd hold back my panic until the movement stopped (it was just a twitch) -and she was still once again. When she'd fall back asleep, I'd lay her in her crib and resume my spot on the rocking chair. I'd watch her sleep until the rest of the house woke up alerting me to the fact that it was officially morning and officially time, once again, to live.

Weeks after the diagnosis, she contracted spinal meningitis. She was hospitalized for ten days. Later she developed RSV, a severe respiratory virus, which meant three nights more in the hospital. And then she caught it again, and again once more. Most of those nights I spent with her in the hospital, which left little time to be home with the other kids. Jason, still a toddler at just two and a half, spent quite a bit of time with my mom which suited him just fine, but for Jessie, who was in kindergarten, those days and nights without me were tough. She missed me, she missed her sister, and she knew just enough to worry.

With the help of some sweet nurses, who worked magic with hospital administrators, a special "girls only" sleep over was arranged. An extra hospital bed, (a huge step up from the window-seat cot I'd been sleeping in) was brought in for Jess and I to share. The bed was placed directly along side the crib where the baby slept. After a night of painting nails, eating pizza and watching movies, Jess fell asleep "in the middle", exactly the place she wanted and needed to be. She slept as close to me as possible, curled up on her side looking at her baby sister, never letting go of the tiny hand she held through the slats of the crib.

Between hospital stays, we took our baby in for bi-weekly brain scans. Oh yeah, remember those? We were still on the look out for sitings of hydrocephalus.

She wasn't feeling well, the day I took her in for a scheduled ultra sound (I suspected another respiratory infection) and noticed, over the shoulder of the lab technician, that something on the scan looked different. The lab tech noticed it too, I could tell by her body language, and by the fact that she stopped talking but continued to take extensive measurements by clicking the buttons on her ultra sound machine. But - she wasn't allowed to tell me anything. Following protocol, she told me the radiologist would contact our pediatrician once he'd read the scan.

I knew enough to know there was something wrong. I was exhausted and scared and I'd had enough. Enough waiting, and enough coming back every two weeks for another scan. I wasn't going home to await the results of this ultra sound. I begged for help. No one in the radiology department would help me; they had rules to follow and they weren't willing to break them even for a sick baby and her just shy of frantic mom. I called our pediatrician from the hallway outside the radiology waiting room, I told him what I saw on the scan, and I told him that my girl was now wheezing with every breath she took. He believed me. He made arrangements right then for my girl to be admitted to the hospital.

She did, in fact, have another case of RSV, and her ventricles as I suspected, were larger than they'd ever been. The pediatrician connected us with the pediatric neurosurgeon, who conferred with me that it was time to stop watching and waiting. Arrangements were made for the shunt surgery to take place as soon the risk of infection from the RSV had passed.

Our girl had been born with many qualities and characteristics that were unusual or out of the norm, tenacity was one of them. At seven months old, respiratory troubles were a thing of the past, she was breathing strong and just weeks away from shunt surgery. At seven months, she was a happy baby whose muscle tone was still very low. She couldn't sit, or roll, or hold her head up while lying on her stomach, but she smiled and she laughed and her eyes were bright.

We were still augmenting her diet with supplements, still unsure how much of them she was actually consuming, and not certain at all if they were making one bit of difference. Oh yeah, remember the metabolic movement disorder? It loomed still, never far from our minds.

And then, one afternoon, while giving my girl a bath, I answered a call from the head metabolic doctor who checked in with us regularly to obtain updated progress information. Mostly, the calls were for clinical reasons, but I was usually eager to speak with this doctor as she was the only one who knew anything at all about the dreaded disorder. Asking if I could call her back at a more convenient time, the doctor told me that she was calling to share some news.

Bath time was over.

I wrapped the baby in a diaper and a towel and laid her in her crib. Grabbing the phone I sat on the sofa in the never used living room to call the doctor back. She had the final lab results, the culture had grown. The results were negative. The hell we'd lived through the last four months was over. The doctor explained that my girl *did not* have the disorder they suspected. She told me though, over the phone, that there was a possibility that she had an even more rare form of the disorder, which they knew even less about. She told me that they'd keep my daughter's tissue sample, and that hopefully one day, when there was more funding, they'd be able to do further research that would provide more information.

That's all.

Congratulations.

Bye-Bye.

No urgent meeting, no face to face.

I sat on the sofa in shock. I was elated, and confused, and overwhelmed.

I called Don, he came home. We danced for joy.

And then, for a few weeks we acted the way normal people with a seven month old might act. We played with our girl and held her without huge fear; we fed her without a huge orange mess. We made no phone calls to doctors, and we did no research into huge diseases we knew little about. We lived in our uncertainty, and we saw that we were okay.

We decided then, it was truly time to stop waiting.

We decided then, it was our thinking that needed to change.

We had exhausted and been exhausted by our search for a diagnosis. We decided to stop the search.

We were ready to let go of the burden of trying to figure out "why" or "what."

We accepted the fact that there would be no quick fix.

We embraced the fact that our girl was unique and that she was uniquely ours.

Our seven-month journey had prepared us for a reality of unknowns. More importantly, our seven-month journey made it clear to us that the "unknowns" are what make the "anythings" possible.

And we were ready for anything.

One month later, in March of 1992, she underwent her first surgery. She was eight months old. We were frightened, but hopeful the shunt would make some kind of difference.

Handing her off to the surgical nurse was hard. The waiting even harder.

The surgeon appeared in the waiting room two hours later with the news that all had gone as planned. The shunt was working. She was in recovery, and we could go see her. He warned us that she may be unhappy coming out of anesthesia, but that she was absolutely fine. His smile grew large when he informed us that he took it upon himself to ensure that only a very small patch of her beautiful head of curls had been shaved.

The walk down the corridor to the recovery room seemed to take forever. We hardly spoke and could barely contain ourselves from shoving past each other and the nurse who escorted us to our precious child. When we saw her at last in a tall metal hospital crib, we stopped in our tracks.

She was dressed in a tiny yellow hospital gown and cream colored knit cap that covered her bandaged head. She was pushing up onto her elbows looking happily around while she lay on her stomach. She was accomplishing, just minutes after surgery, a physical skill that until this point had eluded her. At eight months she was able to lift her head. The surgery had already made a difference!

She looked beautiful and healthy and the smile she wore that day I thought at the time extraordinary. I know now the smile wasn't extraordinary at all. That smile, the smile that had everyone in the recovery room talking, the smile I will never forget, was a glimpse into the resilient, trusting, unafraid, and contented girl she would become.

6

One Year After

HER DEATH TWENTY-TWO years later, although not entirely unexpected, still came as a shock. She struggled with illness and hospitalizations but she'd always been resilient. After each illness or surgery, she went right back to living the life she loved, she was queen of the rebound. —We didn't expect her to die when she did, but she did, and it changed my life irrevocably.

I'm learning to adjust to death's permanent consequences.

In some ways, it's been less of a challenge adjusting to the big obvious emotional things - like the fact that she is never coming back, and that my heart aches when I think about how much I miss her - than it has been adjusting to the things smaller, more subtle, unspoken and everyday.

In the past year, I've learned how to get up in the morning and begin my day without beginning my day taking care of her. I've learned in the past two years how to let go of my daily mothering role, which was something I'd done every day for the past twenty-eight years of my life. My duties as a mother began when my oldest was born and amped up when her brother came along. The care and attention that the two older kids needed from me changed as they grew. They became less dependent on me for their day-to-day needs and looked to me more for advice or a ride to the mall as they got older. The mothering role I provided my youngest went through its changes as she grew too, but she never stopped needing my daily assistance with things like brushing her hair or washing her face or making her dinner. In many ways, I'd been mother to a young child for half of my life.

The past year has allowed me to shift my focus from the acute necessities of the moment. I am getting used to enjoying the flexibility of meandering through a day. I've learned to plan things that I choose to do or be a part of, instead of waking up to figure out where I will be needed. I'm the empty nester grandmother I thought I'd never be able to be. In a little over a year I've just about come to grips with the idea that it's okay to take a walk during the day, and that sitting down to read a book, simply for pleasure in the middle of the afternoon, is okay too.

Spending time without worry is something I'm growing used to.

And I'm figuring out a healthy way to miss my girl.

Determining where and when and how and to whom it feels safe to talk about her is the emotional and social mess I repeatedly find myself in. Sometimes I want to talk about her, and sometimes I don't. Sometimes people want to engage with me, and sometimes they don't. On good days I work at being a student of human behavior, and think carefully before I begin a conversation. On bad days, I have little patience for the effect my story may have on others, and I plunge right in.

I'm learning to read body language and have become pretty adept at weighing reactions that register somewhere on the scale from sorrow, to pity, to concern, to nervous twitches. Sometimes I feel like people are happy, relieved even to acknowledge the elephant in the room. They seem almost grateful for the opportunity to be able to reach out, grab my hand, and gently say, 'I know." Other times it feels like people want to shoo any conversation about her away, afraid that the mention of her name may upset me…or themselves.

For the last twenty-three years, I've tried hard NOT to be known just as The Mom of the Girl With a Disability. I've also tried hard NOT to be known just as The Mom of the Girl Who is Sick, now I try hard NOT to be known just as The Mom of the Girl who has Died. But sometimes I just am The Mom of the Girl With a Disability, Who Got Sick and Died. And sometimes I want to scream it out to make sure everyone knows. I want them to know that she was important and that her life mattered. I want them to know how much we loved her, and how much we hurt in the fact that she's here no more, and by the fact there are people out there that didn't get to know her and won't get to know her, and the very real possibility that she may be forgotten by the people that did.

And through it all, I am adjusting, learning how to be me, without her.

7

Four Years Old

SHE WAS INVITED to a birthday party, her first. Well, it was the first birthday party she'd been invited to all on her own. This wasn't a cousin's party, or a neighbor's party, or a friend of the family's party. This was a preschool friend's party. This was big.... to me. To me, it meant that she'd been accepted and that she was liked. To me it meant the world. To her, it meant that she was invited to a birthday party like all kids were invited to birthday parties. At four years old she was already taking things in stride: happy she'd been invited, but not over the moon about it like I was.

We displayed the girly little invitation atop our kitchen counter for a couple of weeks. We talked about it every morning. We talked about what we thought the party would be like and about who might be there. I was excited for her, and because of that, her excitement grew too, mostly though, I think she was merely indulgent of all the party talk.

The week before the party we made a trip to the toy store to purchase the gift. I wanted the gift to be just perfect, not too much and not too little. A gift that all the kids would think was cool, so they'd think my girl was cool too. All my girl wanted was to finish shopping and go get some lunch. After about an hour of deliberation on just what a four-year-old girl would like, (which I couldn't base solely on what my four year old enjoyed because she gravitated toward things that younger kids preferred like Thomas the Tank Engine or Barney the Dinosaur), we came home with a pink My Little Pony complete with a hairbrush and a fluffy pink satin bed for the Pony to sleep on. I wrapped the gift and took my time doing so in an attempt to make it look awesome, because, you know - my over-eager but less than sensible thought process told me that if the present seemed impressive, then the present-giver would seem impressive too. I wrapped it in festive polka-dot paper and topped it off with a big orange ribbon tied in a bow.

We made a birthday card out of yellow construction paper, and on this, our enthusiasm matched. Making cards was her specialty, she cared about cards and took her time with them. We talked about what she wanted to say, and I wrote it for her in my best kid-friendly handwriting: "I hope your birthday is a fun day. You are so nice. I like to play with you at school." I lightly outlined the letters of her name on the bottom of the card, and she traced over them the best she could. Then she placed a whole bunch of bright rainbow and flower stickers all over the card.

I thought about what she'd wear to the party for days. It didn't matter to her much, but to me of course it did, because, you know, if she looked good people would like her, she'd have lots of friends, and her life would be perfect, right? I asked her if she wanted to wear a dress that used to be her sister's and was one of my favorites—a pale pink seersucker party dress with short capped sleeves and a poufy short skirt. She liked the dress too and said okay. I planned on pulling her long curly hair high into a high ponytail and topping it off just like the present with a long piece of ribbon tied into a pretty bow because that's what you did with little girls' hair in the early '90s. Just thinking about it made me happy.

We talked about how to act and what to do at the party, and we talked about the fact that I wasn't staying. Just dropping her off and then returning a few hours later.

The day of the party finally arrived, and we'd (I'd) talked it to death. There was nothing more I could say or do or control. She looked adorable, and much to my satisfaction, the present did too. We got in the car and drove the half-mile to Danielle's house. I parked the car across the street and held her chubby little hand in mine as we walked up to the front door and rang the bell with anticipation. No one answered. We rang again and waited again. Still no answer. After a few minutes, Danielle and her mom appeared at the door... in their sweatpants. They looked at us, especially at my party-ready girl, and informed us that we were a wee bit early. Twenty- four hours early to be exact. Graciously, they invited us in anyway. We stayed just long enough for me to offer an embarrassed apology, and to explain to the mom, who I didn't know all that well, how much it meant, mostly to me, that my girl had been invited to the party. Hearing her tell the story of just how excited the birthday girl was to extend the invitation caught me by surprise.

Danielle's mom began to talk about the day her daughter checked out "the book". She told of Danielle's excitement about bringing the book home. The book was a book I'd put together at the beginning of the year, and had spiral bound and laminated at Kinko's. The book was an attempt to explain, to the other four-year-olds in my girl's preschool class, how my daughter, who maybe looked a little different than they did, and walked a little different than they did, was also very much like them——and YES, she was different too, and that was okay.

The first few pages of the book focused on similarities and had pages with pictures of our girl playing with her brother and sister, going to the park with her dad, reading stories with me, and coloring.

The middle of the book showed a child's drawing of traced hands (think turkey drawing at Thanksgiving) and focused on differences. Our girl, at four-years-old was healthy, and despite delays in her development, was making great strides. At four-years-old she was happy and alert, and smiley and sweet. She'd just learned to walk. She followed directions well and understood everything we said. At four years old though, our girl spoke only a very few words. At four years old though, our girl was able to use sign language.

Each page from the middle to the end of the book had a picture of her (or her brother or sister) signing a word she used. Each page had a definition, and each page encouraged the kids to try the sign.

The book was fun to make. The book was simple to read. The preschool teachers who embraced my girl also embraced the book. They read it often with the class, and they taught the kids to sign whenever they could. The preschool teachers encouraged the students to check out the book (like a library book) and take it home for a week to share with their family if they wished. Apparently they wished, the book was most often out.

The book was the prompt to the birthday invitation. Danielle loved the book. Danielle loved to sign. Danielle loved to sign with my girl, and according to her mom, Danielle wanted my girl to be her friend.

Hearing Danielle's mom tell how excited her daughter was because *my daughter* was coming to her birthday party made the mistake of arriving at the party an entire day early completely worth it.

Leaving Danielle's house I buckled my pretty little girl back into the car and placed the present on the seat beside her. All dressed up with no place to go, we headed straight for the ice cream shop where we sat across from each other over a big dish of chocolate ice-cream and talked some more about just how great tomorrow would be.

8

Five Years Old

THE YUMMY SMELL of freshly baked brownies filled the kitchen. I added more fluffy powdered sugar to the mixing bowl for the frosting, too much at a time (like I always do) and was covered in a thin layer of the white stuff. I sang along with Natalie Merchant and her clear, sweet voice as it blasted from my stereo speakers and thought about the meeting scheduled for later that afternoon where I'd share, with thanks and celebration, the chocolate goodies I was working on.

The meeting that consumed my thoughts had been planned for several weeks and was the first official progress meeting of the year with my new little kindergartener's teacher, the school principal, and a few others who worked with my girl to help make her days at school successful. The positive news I received on a daily basis via the back-and-forth-book her teacher sent home each afternoon calmed my soul. It was filled with news that allowed me to experience again the luxury of a good night's sleep.

I'd been losing sleep and worrying about the time my youngest daughter would enter the real world of school and the all too real world of big kids for over a year, and worrying, it turns out, was something I was good at. I left no detail behind. I worried how this differently abled, sweet child of mine would physically keep up with her peers. I worried how she'd academically keep up. I worried that she'd have trouble making friends. I worried how other kids would react to her. I worried how they would treat her. I worried that her feelings would get hurt and about the mess she'd make when she ate her peanut butter and jelly sandwich. Would she end up with purple jelly smeared on her lips and cheeks and spend the rest of the day like that because she lacked the ability to competently wipe her own face? Would she get teased for the heavy-footed way she walked, or because she couldn't draw a pretty picture? How would she zip her pants after she went to the bathroom? How would she make it through the day on her own?

These were the worries that filled so many of my nights, these were the worries that the classroom teacher, the classroom aide, and the school occupational therapist quashed for me each evening as I read the day's entry in the back and forth book. They told me that she WAS keeping up (hurray!), and they sent home papers marked with bright red stars and smiley faces on them to prove it. They let me know that she WAS fitting in, that she was invited every day to sit in the middle of all the girls at the lunch table, and that she was never alone on the playground. Each time her new friends Ashley or Brooke called for a play date, the tension that had been gluing my shoulders to my ears for so long loosened, and I found myself breathing a little easier. The meeting later that afternoon had the potential to reduce my stress level far more than any massage appointment or yoga class I'd ever attended. My plan was to leave the meeting later that afternoon feeling absolutely giddy.

I was the last to arrive at the meeting, which was held in an interior windowless conference room at the elementary school. My older kids described this conference room as the place where bad kids and their families had to go to meet with the school principal. The room was void of any real color and had cream paneled walls that were designed to be removed to make the room larger when needed. The walls appeared to be made out of the same laminate material as the top of the too large conference table that filled the space. This room, with its lack of color and décor, felt like a serious place. Still, I was happy to be there armed with my red Tupperware container full of freshly baked brownies.

I took my seat next to a man I'd never met who sat at the head of the table wearing a short-sleeved white shirt. He sat in front of a stack of official-looking papers. His brown hair was slicked back, and he sported a brown homicide detective mustache. He was introduced to me as the school district's psychologist. The four other seats at the table were occupied by the consummate kindergarten teacher, the down-to-earth and logical occupational therapist, the pragmatic school nurse, who I never had too many dealings with except for the occasional call from her telling me I needed to come pick up one of my kids because they were sick (or at least were pretending to be) and the competent-but-jittery school principal, who gave the impression that standardized testing was all she thought about, until the day she revealed to me the agony she was experiencing because her son (who was in middle school) had no friends.

The professionals passed around official looking reports and documents. I passed around brownies and flowered paper napkins. Then we got down to business.

The party line touted by the school principal was that they were "willing" and "eager" to work with our family to make our third child's experience at the school as positive and successful as our first two children's had been. The classroom teacher talked about how delighted she was with my daughter's performance during the first few weeks of school. She shared with the group that my girl was well behaved, that she followed directions, and that for the most part, she was able to participate in class right along with the other kids. She and the occupational therapist described the methods they were using to engage her in learning and socializing. They described her enthusiasm for school, they shared stories of how other students were connecting with her, and they talked of our family's willingness to offer help or suggestions when needed. They said that it was a pleasure to have our girl in class.

The teacher, the therapist and the principal talked of their experience working with other young students with special needs and their families in the past and were confident that those experiences had prepared them to provide the fully inclusive educational setting we were after -one that would allow her to learn, and most important (to me at least) provide opportunities for friendships to develop.

The meeting was going well. I smiled, I nodded and took a bite of my brownie.

Then the man in the white shirt spoke up. He asked us to refer to page five of the paperwork that sat in front of us. He directed our attention to the results of an IQ assessment that showed my girl scoring in the lower-than-one percentile range for children her age. He looked around the table to allow time for that fun fact to sink in, and then explained that he wasn't comfortable allowing her to remain in the regular ed classroom. This school psychologist, who to my knowledge didn't actually know my daughter, was advising that we discuss other options for her schooling based on the few minutes he had spent with her administering his test.

I was against IQ tests and didn't know that one had been given. Doctors and therapists had suggested that an IQ test be performed when she was three years old in an effort to determine her potential, and I'd declined it. Back then, after careful consideration, my husband and I decided against the very real possibility of limitations, either intentionally or unwittingly, being placed on her due to her score. I wasn't interested in allowing expectations to simply be assumed by schoolteachers and administrators. I wanted her to have opportunities to succeed, and even opportunities to fail. I wanted her opportunities to come through experience, I wanted her opportunities to be like everyone else's— limitless.

I was skeptical about the test too. I wondered how a universal test, with universal scoring, could be administered to someone with limited communication and cognitive skills? I wondered how reliable and accurate the test results could be.

Lastly, I wasn't so sure that I wanted to know her IQ score. I was afraid of how knowledge of that number might affect me. I did not want to lose hope.

Hearing now - through the thick fog forming in my brain - this man in the white shirt say that he'd executed an IQ test, and that my girl, who had learned to walk when doctors thought she'd never, who had learned to talk when doctors thought she'd never, who had learned to reason and relate when doctors said she may never, was functioning, according to his test results, at the level of a toddler, was appalling. It was agonizing hearing him say that the regular education classroom was not the place for her, and that based upon his IQ test, she'd be best served in a segregated special education classroom where she'd be able to receive the attention she both needed and deserved.

These weren't the words I'd planned on hearing - this wasn't the way the meeting was supposed to go. The smile had long disappeared from my face. The rest of my brownie remained uneaten on the flowered napkin in front of me.

I felt like I'd just been socked in the gut, which unfortunately was a feeling I was familiar with. In the five years I'd been a mother to this child with special needs, I'd been slammed by that feeling more than once. Like the time shortly after she was born when a misguided family member suggested that we institutionalize our baby, or the time when she was a toddler sitting with me in the waiting area of our pediatrician's office, and I heard a mother tell her child not to stare. And then there's the time another out-of-touch relative stood over her hospital crib and called her his little hero before running out the door to catch a plane for a European vacation. Each time that feeling slammed into me, I became stronger despite the pain or emotion it caused. Those socks in the gut confirmed to me that my priority was to care for this daughter of mine who couldn't care for herself.

When the man in the white shirt condescendingly placed his hand on my shoulder and asked me if I was going to be okay, I immediately knew that I would be. The cramped conference room was no place for a meltdown, nor was there time for one either. There'd be plenty of time for that later once I was safely home behind closed doors. At that moment, with the man's hand on my shoulder, I refused to allow myself to be discredited by my emotions. Stuffing the impulse to shove the school psychologist and his official looking papers out the door of the conference room, I knew it was time to be strong for my girl.

With emerging confidence, I adamantly stated to the little group seated around me that I was unaware and unhappy that the school had taken it upon themselves to run an IQ test. Without hesitation, the man in the white shirt slid a piece of paper in front of me showing my big loopy signature beneath a bunch of typed words. Those typed words included a phrase about the school being able to perform whatever tests they deemed necessary to determine my daughter's placement in the school. I'd signed this document earlier that spring during school registration just days after my mother had died. My signature gave the school the go-ahead. I was a rookie, and I'd made a rookie mistake. I should have questioned just which types of tests could be included in the "might be deemed necessary" category.

Stepping back up to the plate, this time like a seasoned veteran, I asked this man in the white shirt how much time he'd spent with my daughter. I asked him if he had developed a rapport with her before he sat, as a clinician, across from her at a little table to administer his big test. After confirming the fact that the only time he'd spent with her was in testing mode for an hour or so, I asked him if he thought the kid we had been discussing in the meeting had sounded to him like the kid described by his test results? I asked him how, according to her menial IQ, he thought it even possible that this new little kindergartener, on her own, found her way into the building, and through the halls to her classroom? I asked him how he found it even possible that she could hang up her backpack in the spot designated just for her, and then take her place in the classroom, which included finding the desk that was meant just for her, the desk with her name boldly written across it in impeccable teacher handwriting?

On a roll and not really waiting for an answer from the man in the white shirt, I confirmed the fact that the best kindergarten teacher on the planet was happy to have my girl in her classroom, and that the realistic occupational therapist thought it the place for her as well. They both agreed, that with modifications that they were willing to make she could keep up with the work. They believed that the regular ed classroom would provide the best opportunity to learn positive new skills that would transfer to the real world.

The school nurse, who really had no dog in this fight but was required to be at the meeting for legal, cross-your-T's-and-dot-your-I's reasons, said she had no problem with our girl's placement in the regular ed classroom.

I looked next to the nervous principal (who had the difficult job of both protecting district employees and mitigating anxious parents), she gave me a nod and a small smile and the courage to continue.

Admitting that I'd made a mistake by signing the document allowing any and all testing, I asked for a blank piece of paper. With a shaking hand I began to write out a statement that denied the man in the white shirt, or any other district psychologist, in any color of shirt, future access to my daughter without my prior approval. In addition, I added a declaration that I wanted the IQ test and its results removed from her permanent school record.

With false confidence, I added my signature to the bottom of the page and asked everyone at the table to sign as well. I passed the form counterclockwise first to the teacher who was sitting on my right; she signed then passed the form along. I watched as each person around the table followed suit until the paper lay in front of the person seated to my left. Whether it was out of agreement, defeat, or the surest way to get me off his caseload, the man in the white shirt picked up the pen and signed his name.

The professionals packed up their paperwork.

I packed up my remaining brownies and napkins and headed home for a good cry.

The man in the white shirt was never again seen by any member of my family.

Her IQ scores were removed from her record.

She remained in the regular ed classroom.

9

Eight to Ten Years Old

MY FIRST MARRIAGE ended in divorce. It was headed that direction long before the birth of our third child, but when she was born and born with disabilities to boot, divorce was something we just didn't have time for.

We spent our time instead, searching for the parenting guidebook that didn't exist. The one that would teach us everything we needed to know about raising a child with a disability— a disability that had no name, which made our task even harder. Eventually, through trial and error, and research of disabilities that did have names, we took what information we were able to glean and came up with a way to parent and nurture our child with disabilities and her siblings that was right for all of us. Our family was suddenly different, different from most of the families we knew and different from what we had planned. Disability was here with us to stay, and we accepted it completely, but our ultimate goal was to eliminate disability's possible overtake of our family. Our focus was on raising well-adjusted children.

We devoted ourselves to our kids. We worked hard to make

sure that the older two wouldn't feel slighted or resent the fact that they had a sister who required so much attention, and we searched for every opportunity we could find to help our youngest one thrive. Despite the challenging medical and social issues our family faced, and the underlying struggles of our marriage, we were unified in our desire to make sure that each of our kids lived typical kid lives.

As parents, we dove full on into the roles and patterns we'd established. I concentrated my efforts wholly on the kids, running the household, and learning the world of disability. Don kept his focus on the financial health of our family. We divided and conquered, each doing what we did best without much overlap or collaboration.

When our youngest turned eight, and our lives had fallen into a more predictable routine, we found ourselves finally able to come up for air. We looked at the life and at the family that we'd created; we were proud and delighted that each of our kids were good kids and they were thriving. We took heart in the easy way they all got along, and in the protective way they looked out for each other. Jess and Jason had perfected the art of loving their sister, with just the right amount of coddling and teasing, and she in turn, without a doubt, knew the two of them hung the moon. Eight years later our kids were leading the kind of happy, full lives we'd hoped they would.

Eight years later though, Don and I were tripping over the issues we'd tried to sweep under the rug for too long. Eight years later, when we took the time to look at us, we found there was no us. We ended our marriage a year after that.

We'd successfully hidden our unhappiness from the kids (if that's something that can be chalked up in the successful column), who were crushed by the news of our divorce. Understandably, they were undone, the two older ones especially, who were sad, with a little helping of something else on the side. Jessie added a portion of angry to her plate, and Jason, an order of fear. At times they shut me out while they struggled with what their parents had done to them, and at times I was nearly suffocated with their emotional needs.

During those divorce years though, the youngest child, the one who had always needed me the most, suddenly became the child who needed me the least. She was sad too sometimes, usually when she saw that her brother and sister were sad. Mostly she was confused by the changes, and challenges, that were occurring; "Why does Dad live somewhere else, why do I have to sleep there sometimes too, and why are you the one cutting the grass, Mom?"

Of all of us though, she was the one who found it easiest to adjust and carry on. She relied heavily those years on her ability to worry not, which was the superpower she'd been born with. I'd seen her use this greatest of all superpowers many times in the past, at scary doctor's appointments, at blood draws, or in social situations where she might be in over her head. I'd seen her use her superpower when she attempted some new physical challenge, but I honestly don't think I'd ever been more grateful for its presence in her life than during those divorce years.

She knew just how to use it too, and its implications were far-reaching. She used it to bring levity to situations and to show us alternative ways of coping. She didn't analyze or overthink her own actions or the actions of those around her, and because of that, she was the person each member of our family most wanted to be with. Because she worried not (which freed me from worrying about her) my load was lessened, and I had more time to focus on Jessie and Jason who were struggling.

She was also healthy those years. There were no medical concerns or doctor's appointments - only routine therapy that, honestly, felt like a respite for me. Her physical and occupational therapy appointments became the highlights of my week. We were out of the house and focused on something other than divorce. She was fun and easy to be with. She accepted and loved me because I was her mom and I was good to her. She didn't question my motives and actions or make me feel guilty about my life choices and how they'd affect her. She trusted me and knew that I'd take care of her; she knew her dad would too.

A year passed, and again my little family had adjusted to something new. Surprisingly, single parenting was far less difficult than I'd imagined. Having only myself to get things done, I did them. The kids settled in and let go of their sadness and most of their sides. Remnants of anger and fear still lingered, but for the most part, were gone. Together we'd worked through them; we were living a new normal. It was good.

My plan was to remain single, and then I met Curt, who in another year would change my mind about that.

The kids were ten, twelve, and sixteen, and knew very little about Curt until our relationship got serious. The only one excited or particularly interested to even meet him was the ten-year-old. She was also the only one who allowed herself to like him from the get-go. She met him in her usual fashion, without trepidation or judgment and took to him because he was kind and because I liked him too.

The other kids were a harder sell. They'd gotten used to things the way they were and liked them that way. A mom who dated was kind of gross, a mom who dated wasn't what they had in mind. And then there was the simple fact that they weren't too keen on allowing a stranger access to our new little family unit of four.

We took things slow and spent time primarily with the youngest daughter who was around the most and was most interested in spending time with us. Her enthusiasm for Curt helped the other two come around. Her stories at the dinner table of what Curt had done or said to her had the kids listening. They were impressed with the way he treated her; I was impressed by the way he treated her. Jess, Jason and I had never discussed it, and probably at that point in our lives didn't even know that our opinions of people were based largely upon how they interacted with our girl. Treat her right, and you've won a place in our heart, ...treat her poorly, and you're OUT. Our girl herself was giving this new guy in her life the thumbs up, Jess and Jason took notice and allowed themselves to get to know him too.

Curt and I were married the next year. The kids were happy but understandably still carried with them their unique little sides of something else. Jason, the middle child, cried at our wedding; his tears a mixture of joy and fear. Jess, the oldest sang a beautiful song at our wedding about being loved forever. She sang pretty and sweet, but I'm sure, couldn't help but wonder, what had happened to love the first time around. And the youngest—the one armed with her superpower, she glowed at our wedding, first holding my hand, then Curt's, and then the hands of her brother and sister. She wore a grin that night, a grin so sweet I'll never forget. She wore that night a grin that embodied contentment.

10

Eight Years Old

SHE WAS EIGHT years old the day our occupational therapist brought out the big kid bike and asked her if she wanted to ride. The bike was light blue and equipped with training wheels. By that point, she'd just about mastered the skill of peddling a preschooler's plastic Big Wheel up and down the sidewalk. I thought the therapist was crazy by asking her to try something so far outside her ability level and comfort zone, but he'd worked magic with my girl through the years, so I kept my mouth shut, and I watched her eyes light up when she caught sight of the sparkly silver streamers that hung from the bike's handlebars.

She said yes—she wanted to try to ride the shiny blue bike. Of course, she did. When someone she loved and trusted presented her with an idea, gave her instruction or asked her to try something new -she always said yes, she always joined, she always tried. And once she started, she didn't quit. She believed in herself, and she believed in the people in her life. She never, even when she was of legal age, smoked a cigarette or took a sip of alcohol, she would never think of kissing a boy, and she'd never run by the pool. She was a rule follower who liked to follow directions to a T. I don't know if she was, like Lady Gaga says, "Born That Way," or if her determination was a behavior learned from the hours and hours of therapy she endured from a very early age.

Her occupational and physical therapists were gentle taskmasters who helped her figure out how to move more effectively. A child with low tone puts a lot of energy into getting muscles to fire. Her therapists were the people who were able to teach her how to outsmart some of the limitations placed on her by her low tone and her developmental delays. These were the people who helped her begin to navigate the world with some independence. They taught her to thrive in a world that wasn't built for people like her, a world with stairs and uneven surfaces, a world with escalators and heavy doors — a world where conformity is the norm, a world that can be unforgiving to people with differences.

Left to my own selfish devices, it's entirely possible that I would have simply done everything for her myself, which would have spared me the agony of watching her struggle with things like reaching for a toy that was just out of range, or trying to put on her shoes and socks, or navigating a flight of stairs. Doing everything for her would have saved me time too, but doing everything for her would have taught her nothing but dependency. We sought the advice of therapists, who worked with our girl, therapists who, in reality, worked with our whole family. They taught us how to live with changed expectations, and showed us how it was possible to still expect the best. They taught each of us how to be patient, how to be persistent, and how much power there was in determination.

When she was just a toddler, her therapists taught her how to get the most out of every movement she made and how to ignite and shut down her muscles, a skill that typically comes naturally. Their work to develop efficient and effective movement often meant a change in the way she instinctively did things- (think golf pro changing your golf grip, or being forced to write with your non-dominant hand). Sometimes frustration got the best of her, and her eyes would fill with tears. Our dedicated therapists never quit though: they kept her engaged with their exceptional creativity, their praise, and their encouragement. They taught her that giving up wasn't an option. They knew just how far they could push her and kept her engaged. As her mom, sitting on the sidelines in her therapy sessions, it wasn't always easy to watch, but seeing her satisfaction when she finally held, in her chubby little hand, the toy her therapist had her working so hard to reach by leaning and twisting just the right way, made me whoop and holler with joy. Each time she successfully lifted the white porcelain teapot with two hands and pretended to pour tea (which was really Kool-Aide) without spilling, pride filled the room. She was four-years-old the day the physical therapist asked me to stand near the door of the therapy room while she supported and encouraged my girl to take a few steps using a silver aluminum walker (the kind made for old people, but tiny), it was impossible to tell which of us was most thrilled with her accomplishment.

Those therapists worked with her diligently for years. They saw her, twice a week when she was a baby and throughout her toddler years in our home. We started early on, with physical and occupational therapy, then we added speech therapy somewhere along the way until therapy became a way of life for her. Other kids went to gymnastics classes; she went to therapy. The therapists encouraged her brother and sister to come to therapy with her when they could and even encouraged the kids to bring their friends along too, which made it all so fun. With the big kids there our girl tried harder and reveled in the fact that she could be the one to show everyone just what to do and just how to do it. The big kids experienced first hand how hard she worked, and they grew in their understanding that sometimes the best thing they could do for their sister was to encourage her to try things on her own. Watching the way the three kids or the three kids plus friends laughed easily together and took part in whatever therapy games or activity the therapist had planned for the day filled my heart to overflowing.

Those therapists were so smart and made all the difference for us in the early years. Because our ultimate goal, as she grew older, was that she become an active and happy part of the real world, we began meeting our therapists at the grocery store or our favorite park and even her school. The therapists worked with her in all these places and instilled in her a sense of confidence and independence. The work was hard. She rarely complained, she never cried, she always tried.

Obviously, it should have come as no surprise to me that she agreed to try to ride the big blue bike when the therapist showed it to her. Together they worked for months on skills like core strength, endurance, and cognitive awareness until she had the ability to position and balance her body independently. The occupational therapist started by getting her on the bike with its training wheels attached. Then he moved on to balancing games and exercises while the bike stood indoors on a stand. He then moved on to balancing the bike outside next to a curb, and on and on and on. Her therapist never failed to come up with new ideas that would build her confidence, and she never gave up trying. I kept my skepticism to myself, but I believed that the two of them were working hard toward an unattainable goal.

There were days I used the time she spent at therapy to run errands. One day, pulling back into the parking lot of the therapist's office, where I'd left the two of them working, I spotted them waiting for me with Cheshire Cat grins on their faces. They were waiting to show me that she could finally do it. SHE COULD RIDE. She rode that big blue bike with the silver streamers hanging from the handlebars (minus the training wheels) around and around the parking lot, while I stood there next to the therapist with my mouth wide open. She was almost ten years old.

The next afternoon we made a colorful flyer on the computer. It showed a stick figure girl wearing a red dress, riding a blue stick figure bike. There was a stick figure sun in the corner, and words printed across the middle of the flyer proclaiming the exciting news that she could ride a bike. We invited our family and friends and our entire neighborhood to our house to celebrate. We had a cake that looked just like the flyer.

Fifty people lined our street and stood in our driveway the day of the party. Her therapist helped her put her helmet on and mount the beast. No one made a sound. I was a nervous wreck, and so proud of her I thought I'd burst. I was concerned she'd fall and hoped she'd hold it together in front of so many people. I silently prayed for her success and held my breath when the therapist gave her a gentle push. She wobbled a little and then through partially closed eyes, I saw her push her glitter blue tennis shoes down hard onto the pedals of the bike and take off, through her admirers, for a triumphant ride up the street.

The crowd went wild.

11

Nine Years Old

SHE WAS THIRTEEN months old when, after some cognitive testing, the local government agency that provided help for people with disabilities deemed her eligible to receive their services. Services meant, among other things, that she could participate in therapy programs offered by the county, that we'd have access to different types of funding to help pay for things like medication, equipment, and respite care, and that when she became an adult, the agency would help us fund and find independent living for her if that's what we wanted.

Eligibility sounded great until I learned how ridiculously underfunded the agency was, and that all "eligibility" actually meant was that her name would be placed in the queue and that the wait time for services would be approximately ten years.

It was a farce, but a farce I was willing to play along with especially when I looked to the future and wondered what her life might look like when she was an adult. If there were supports out there that would help her live independently, I was determined to ensure that she'd have access to those supports, especially if those supports would enable her to live and thrive as an adult even after we were gone.

I placed her name on the waitlist and was assigned a case manager. We met once a year at a coffee shop or talked once a year over the phone. She took copious notes while we talk-ed to record any changes in my daughter's health and to doc-ument my girl's developmental progress. The case manager always ended our conversations by asking me what more the agency could do for us. My answer, because of the wait list and the fact that we were not receiving any tangible services, was always "everything."

Each year, the case manager, whose fault this was not, tried to assuage my frustration by telling me that since we were of-ficially clients of the agency - if we ran into a real emergency requiring significant technical or financial assistance (like a communication device or a remodeling of our home for added accessibility) - we would have access to funding. My yearly phone call or meeting with the case manager was like an insurance policy that held our place in line for the future and offered the promise of help if things got worse.

Because our contact with the agency was minimal and some-what perfunctory, I was caught off guard when my girl turned nine years old, and I received a letter stating that her eligi-bility was up for redetermination. The letter noted that the agency would be sending someone over for a reassessment and that the meeting would last no longer than twenty min-utes. The need for a reevaluation was based upon the fact that my girl's disability had no official name; therefore, she had no official diagnosis. Her re-evaluation would be to confirm that my daughter still showed signs of mental retardation. Ouch.

For nine years, we'd worked tirelessly to diminish, overlook, get past, overcome, and work with the real fact that she was mentally retarded. Although we refused to allow her IQ score to become a part of her official record, we acknowledged that she learned differently and sometimes slowly. We acknowledged the fact that she needed extra help, and we recognized that, in so many ways, she was different from her peers. But, that's not what we dwelled on. We focused instead on highlighting her strengths and developing new methods of learning. As true as we knew it to be, we never used the words mental retardation.

The logic I'd used in disallowing her IQ score to become public record (the logic of not wanting to limit her or label her) which by the way, was a logic I still firmly believed in, was at this juncture hurting us. An official IQ score that would allow her to be judged and placed neatly into a category was precisely what we needed, and precisely what I was still not going to allow.

Proving her eligibility without an official diagnosis or an official IQ "score" was going to take some doing.

I needed to prepare for the assessment. I did not want her to be kicked off that waiting list.

The preparation was sobering and counterintuitive and hurt like hell. I'd forgotten how to look for her weaknesses and hated thinking about how very far behind her peers she really was. Nevertheless, because I knew it was necessary, I pulled out a piece of paper and began to compile a list of her deficiencies:

*   can't tie her shoes

* can't count coins
* can't tell time
* can't read at grade level (or the level below that, or even the level below that)
* can't do a somersault
* can't add without counting out loud
* can't keep up academically with her 3rd-grade peers (without major curriculum modifications)
* can't keep up socially with 3rd-grade peers (or 2nd-grade peers for that matter)
* can't brush her hair or teeth
* knows that beef comes from a cow, and pork from a pig, but can't grasp the fact that chicken comes from a chicken

Next, I contacted her pediatrician, her therapists, and her classroom teachers and asked them if they'd come up with lists of the weaknesses they observed.

The day of the evaluation, I woke with a headache. There was no school that day, teacher conferences or something. The older kids slept in while their younger sister lay sprawled in her pajamas, watching cartoons on the family room floor. Her curly hair was in crazy bed-head fashion, and her rosy wet lips still held the faintest residue of the scrambled eggs she'd eaten at breakfast. With the tenacity of a mother who believes she's doing what is best for her child, I talked myself out of cleaning her up or getting her dressed. I wanted her to have a certain look about her, mentally retarded was the look I was going for, but unsure how to achieve. And I thought that distracting her during the assessment, by keeping the TV on and tuned to cartoons wasn't a bad idea either.

The social worker rang the doorbell.

I had not told my girl who was coming or why. I had not prepared her in any way, except to tell her that the lady at our door had come to meet her and ask a few questions. We all sat down at the kitchen table, and I just let my girl be herself. She was shy and a little nervous. She acted silly and hid behind my sleeve a lot. When she had trouble answering the social worker's question she'd look to me for help that I didn't give, which was excruciating. When she got bored with the conversation, her eyes wandered to the TV. She wasn't very compliant, and I sat there and let it happen. It was humiliating. It was the antithesis of the way I'd done things for the last nine years.

After she answered several questions and told the social worker she wanted to be a fireman when she grew up, she officially ended the interview by wandering over to the sofa where she sat down to play with some toys and watch her cartoon. I didn't stop her; I just let her go.

I gave the social worker the lists I'd made of all the things my girl couldn't do, and then to make things perfectly clear I handed her all the notes I'd received from the pediatrician and the therapists that backed up my disparaging appraisal of the child I was profoundly proud of everyday of her life, despite the information the papers held.

The therapist told me I'd done good work. I told her I hated doing the work I'd done.

The social worker, who was probably all of twenty-five years old, turned and asked me what I envisioned when I thought about my daughter's future. Wanting our meeting to come to an end, I told her I didn't know. Pushing a bit she ventured to say that surely I'd thought about what the future held for my girl —and admittedly I had, thousands of times, but sharing my deepest, darkest fears with this woman, just doing her job, who came to my house looking for proof that my daughter was mentally retarded, wasn't something I felt like doing.

I held back the tears along with the truth that thinking about her future made me sad, and anxious, and that thinking about her future sometimes made me grieve the typical future she most likely wouldn't have. You know - the future where she'd grow up, go to college, get a job, find someone to love, settle down, have kids of her own and live happily ever after. Taking a deep breath, I told the social worker that I'd discovered it was sometimes best, as a parent of a child with a disability, not to allow yourself to think too far ahead.

My girl who sat nearby still watching cartoons hardly noticed when the social worker said good-bye. Instead of requesting that she turn the TV off and walk our guest to the door with me, I let her keep watching, all this of course, in the name of keeping up the mentally retarded act.

Closing the door as the social worker walked down our front porch steps, the words and sentiment I should have spoken came to mind too late. What I should have said was, that whatever path our girl's future took, her future would be just fine. We'd make sure of it.

I should have told the social worker that I was resentful over the way I'd prepared for our meeting, and how disappointed I was in myself for the way I'd neglected to talk about the incredible strides my girl had made in the nine years she'd been on the planet. I should have told her how ashamed I was - of myself - for allowing my daughter to appear both physically and socially unkempt.

I should have told her that my daughter's future was going to be bright—-because we'd help her build a future based not upon her weaknesses but upon her strengths.

I should have said all that, but I didn't. The social worker was gone.

A few days later I received a letter in the mail informing me that our girl had again been deemed eligible for services. Her name would remain on the waitlist. She had qualified, because she was, in fact, mentally retarded.

I wiped my eyes and thought about how uncomfortable it was to see the words "mental retardation" (no matter how accurate) typed next to the name of my sweet, sweet child.

And that's when I knew it was time to stop - time for me to stop; stop being sad, and stop being resentful. It was time for me to focus again on the "coulds." It was time for the "could nots" to take their rightful place somewhere behind the scenes.

Brushing myself off, I placed the letter of reinstatement into a file marked "Things I Never Want to Look At Again But Think I Should Keep" when the last line of the letter caught my eye, "eligibility will be redetermined again on or before her 14th birthday."

12 | Eighteen Months After

WEEKS GO BY for me now, and I don't encounter anyone with significant disabilities. This used to be the world I inhabited; now it's just the world I observe. Where had they all disappeared to these last 18 months? Were they there and I just didn't see them? Were they there and I just didn't want to see them? They had to have been - there are an estimated 24.1 million people living in the US with a severe disability. Let's just say, for sake's saying, that these folks were equally spread across all 50 states. That would mean that my state would have 480,000 people here with some weighty issues. While not a huge number (in Colorado that makes up about 9% of the population) you'd think I'd have seen a few of these people around here somewhere, but I didn't, or at least I didn't acknowledge that I did.

The weeks before Christmas this year though, things were different. I couldn't escape it. Everywhere I went, I saw someone with a disability and not just any someone. It seemed that every someone I saw was a young adult between the ages of 20 and 30 years old who reminded me of my youngest daughter, the daughter whose life was laced and woven so tightly with my own for many reasons. Was that because she lacked the skills she needed to navigate the world around her, or did the world around her fail to acquire the skills it needed to navigate her? At any rate, around Christmas time this year, I was constantly reminded of the daughter who a year and a half ago, in early spring, had died.

The grocery store was overflowing with folks overfilling their buggies with food for the holidays. The atmosphere in the shops this time of year, while cramped and crowded, makes me sort of giddy and warm with remembered feelings. Working at a mall in high school and through college breaks at Christmas, I was always a sucker for the hustle and bustle of it all, helping people choose the perfect gift (and back in the day when stores offered that sort of thing) taking the time to wrap it just so. Even listening to people complain about all they had to do was more than okay with me; in fact, I enjoyed it. People walking around wearing their winter coats and hats, Christmas music playing, snow boots tracking in the slush from the parking lot, darkness falling early, headlights reflecting off the wet roads that my dad drove me home on after work because he was the kind of dad that did that kind of thing, and family and friends coming home - these are memories that I work never to forget.

It was this feeling that pulled me through the crowded market as I shopped for my family's holiday dinner this year. I had a list and was racing through the narrow aisles. Taking a sharp left turn, I literally ran into a young man trying to pilot his buggy in the busy store too. I apologized and looked up, expecting to be scowled at for not looking where I was going. Instead, I was met with smiling eyes and a sweet face telling me that I was okay, that there was no problem, and that I should have a very merry Christmas. The fact that he told me, "You're okay" was a fact not lost on me. The young man who told me this had Down's syndrome. The young man was assuring me! I loved his confidence; I loved that he was on his own, living his life, shopping with independence, enjoying it, and engaging in it. His certainty was profound. I thought about him throughout the day. His two words, "you're okay," spoke volumes. To me, "you're okay" meant ALL was okay— he was okay, I was okay, the daughter I lost was okay, and all the rest of it was okay too. Far too much meaning heaped into those two words and that smile, I know, but his presence there at just that time was no coincidence. It just wasn't; I don't believe in coincidence. He was supposed to be there on that day, at that time, in that exact grocery store aisle and so was I.

Taking our grandson to a holiday movie, at the local theater, we waited for a group of people to cross the street in front of our car. The ground was snowy, the lights from the cars and those of the decorated trees and buildings nearby reflected off each other and our windshield creating a magical winter scene. All around us, people were walking; the ice rink was full of skating kids, and the sticky sweet smell of roasted nuts mingled with voices that carried through the cold night air. Stopping at a crosswalk waiting for a group of people to pass in front of our car, I noticed that they moved slowly and then took note that one in the group helped another along by holding her arm at the elbow to guide her safely across the street, just the way we used to guide our sweet girl safely across the street and safely across her life. I miss that holding on thing. The girl they were helping turned her head to look left, and as our eyes met, she smiled. Her face was somehow different;

her walk a bit off balance; she had a disability, and she was smiling, and she was happy. I was teary and surprised and overtaken by a feeling of enormous loss, for both my girl and for the way I cared for her. It was not a coincidence that her smiling eyes caught mine.

Our girl loved to eat out, and she loved to go to the same places over and over again. Familiar settings were her thing, especially when people knew her and were kind to her. There were a few places in town she was sure she had attained superstar status. One of these places was a family owned pizza shop that we began going to when she was just a baby. From the owner joking around with her and seeming very pleased to see her each and every time she came in, to the bartender filling her glass with so many red cherries there was barely any room for the Sprite she ordered because that's the way she liked it, this was her "Cheers" - a place where everyone knew her name, where she was accepted and comfortable. This was a place that after her death I avoided like crazy. This was the place (because it was convenient) Curt and I decided to go one night just before Christmas to grab a pizza.

Curt walked ahead of me following the hostess when someone caught his attention. He stooped for a minute to chat and laugh with a young woman and the older couple she was with. We eventually were seated in the booth just behind these people. When I asked Curt if he knew them, he said he didn't and asked me if I did. I looked more carefully and saw that the young woman, their daughter, had...... wait for it, you know it's coming......... disabilities. We know lots of families with kids with disabilities, but we did not know these people.

The young woman was friendly and wanted to talk to someone, so she chose Curt; everybody does, everybody ALWAYS does, he's one of those guys that people are just drawn to. He's got the energy for it, and really, he's so much nicer than I am. Sometimes I don't pay much attention to whom he's talking, as was the case that night, until he asked me to take a closer look. Then, I could not tear my eyes away.

Waiting for our order, I tried not to stare, which was no easy task. I had a direct view of the parents every time I looked up. Stealing glances, I saw how tired the mother looked. The lines on her face were deep; her eyes lacked sparkle, the straight line her lips made was without expression. The dad too seemed old, although I couldn't see his face as much because he kept it pointed down most of the time, toward his food. The daughter, who was probably about 25, had long blond hair held up in a half pony with an elastic band. Her outfit, while put together, was not something a typical woman her age would wear. She had on a powder blue windbreaker, a small-printed floral shirt, jeans, and big white tennis shoes. No one was talking much at their table. The few times I did notice conversation, it was the daughter talking while the mom looked into her daughter's eyes nodding her head. They didn't smile; they mostly ate in silence. My heart ached for the mother and father, my heart ached for the girl, and at the same time, my heart was exploding with love and gratitude for my husband, who knows just how to connect with people and make them feel special.

I sat in the booth at the table behind the family that wasn't talking much, remembering the joy my husband brought to my girl's life, and how much she adored him. They loved each other big, always doing something to make the other happy, and scheming to take some burden off me, by running errands together in the afternoons or working on secret projects in the garage. Remembering all of this, I watched the family in the booth and was grateful that their girl recognized in an instant the kind of man I get to call my husband. He made her smile, and he made her parents smile. I wished we could have somehow brought them into our conversation, but we didn't. I was sad for this exhausted family, and imagined, not very optimistically, that they saw their future as one Groundhog Day after another...where nothing but their age would change from year to year.

Bundled up this morning to continue some Christmas shopping, it came at me again out of nowhere, like it always does, unannounced and stealthily. Browsing in a busy shop, I move aside to let someone pass, and I see them, a mother pushing her adult son in a reclining wheelchair. My heart pounds at the sight, I want to talk to them, I want to touch the handles of the wheelchair, I want to hold the mother's hand and tell her that I understand her life. I want to talk to the son and make sure he is being loved and cared for and adored. I want to help her maneuver, I want to hug them, I want them to hold me, and I want to cry in the son's lap, and in the mother's arms. Instead, I watch and follow them around acting like I'm just browsing, until I finally can follow them no more without the risk of being discovered. I try to do the shopping I set out to do. Looking at everything to find just the right little treats that I'm sure I care about way more than my grown-up kids do, I keep reaching for the things that I'd buy for the daughter who isn't here anymore, the things I'd buy for the daughter who isn't coming back. Remembering the pure joy that a package of peppered salami could bring, I recognize that Sad starts to fill my chest. This time though, it's a Sad that I'm sort of okay with, it's a nostalgic and cozy kind of Sad that wraps me up and reminds me to feel.

Sloppy parking lot successfully negotiated, car packed with Christmas goodies, sliding into the driver's seat ready to move on, I see the mom and son duo, and it happens all over again. I'm frozen. I can't move. I stare and watch as she performs all the steps just she knows how to do, to get her big heavy son and his big heavy chair into her big heavy car, which she has no choice but to drive, when probably she longs for a little two-seater convertible. I watch as others watch her and know how you simply keep going to avoid the stares, and act like what you're doing is the most normal thing in the world to be doing, and oh, also the easiest— like everyone does this all the time, what's the big deal? I watch as she first puts in the bags, then starts the car to warm it up for them, I watch him as he patiently waits for her knowing she will help him, she always does, she will get it done, she will make him comfortable, she will do whatever it takes. I watch her begin to move his substantial body; I want to rush over and do it for her, do it with her, I want to tell someone, anyone, that yes, it's okay, to offer her a hand- she'll take it if she needs. I watch a while more until tears flood my eyes and I can no longer see.

Pushing Sad away I hurry to meet Curt for a quick lunch. I'm good at pushing Sad away; it's one of the things you learn to do after the death of a child. Sad is used to being pushed around by me, but like the playground punk, knows it can hold its foot out to trip me anytime it sees the opportunity, which is what happens the minute I walk in the door of the restaurant. The same restaurant, which, of course, on this day is the restaurant a group of adults with disabilities and their caretakers stop for lunch.

I see them, and the frozen thing creeps up on me again, but this time it's not as strong. I'm not compelled to talk with each and every one of these people. Maybe it's because they are with their caretakers and not their mothers, and maybe it's because I'm kind of tapped out from my recent experiences. I watch their interactions with each other and with their caretakers. I watch and wonder if they are happy. I watch the silence of one man as he looks in a lunch box (that most likely his mother packed for him) and wonder how many lunches that mother must have made for this probably 40-year-old man/boy/son. I watch as a caretaker straightens the hat of a fun looking man waiting to order, and am delighted by her small act of affection - happy that the man has someone who tenderly and playfully looks out for him.

I tell my husband about the day so far. He asks me what I'm feeling looking at the people in the restaurant. I say that I'm worn out and sad—sad for them. (If someone had told me they were sad for our girl when she was alive, I would have been hurt and would have boldly defended her quality of life.) He, the husband I am so lucky to have, quickly reminded me of the happy life that she, the daughter we were so blessed to have, led.

We sit in our booth at the restaurant and talk about how much she would have enjoyed a morning shopping with her mom or a noontime lunching with friends. We talk about how she didn't possess the unhappy gene, and how Happy was her default. We talk about how she didn't really even know Sad, and about just how beautiful all of that was.

Of the 48,000 people with severe disabilities that could potentially live in my state, the weeks surrounding Christmas made me feel like I saw most of them. They were not the ones in hiding for a year and a half - I was. I think I was being shown that Christmas, that it was time to start moving forward, and moving forward didn't mean leaving the people I'd forever be drawn to behind. It was time again to begin to see.

Being now, on the outside of the disability world and looking in, feels voyeuristic, and lonely, and safe, and thoughtful, and sad, and hopeful and grateful and a whole bunch of other emotions I can't even begin to recognize or name. Re-entering normal life, which is what is expected and what one eventually does after loss, requires a lot of pushing Sad down and a lot of forcing Happy up. The reality is that I'm glad Sad is still around; I don't want it to consume me, but I don't want it to leave me either.

Sad for me, includes the happy memories of a life lived too quickly, and Sad has a way of keeping that short life alive. The Sad is there because she is gone, but the Happy remains because she was.

13

Two Years After

THE LITTLE RED iPad sprang to life again the day my eighty-two-year-old-dad began talking about getting one of those "screen-type-tablet-things that you tap with your finger." He said he wanted to replace his slow-moving "machine" and was referring to the machine that others would commonly call a computer. Wanting to see if Dad could use an iPad, I went to find the only one we had in the house, the one our girl kept on the desk in her room (which was the room that, despite our best attempts of turning it into a family room, will forever be thought of and simply called, her room).

The built-in desk that remains in that room is still home to her jewelry, her markers, some old cards and letters, a container full of big brightly colored beads with extra large holes for stringing, and the beloved little iPad, with its dirty red cover, which I placed back on her desk a month or so after she died and haven't touched since. I've thought about clearing her things from the top of that desk, the last spot in our house that remains just the way she left it, but all I can do is think about it. I can't bring myself to action. I'm not ready yet, so I leave it.

The necessity of giving my dad a shot at using an iPad before he went out and bought one had me sitting down at the little desk tucked into the corner of her room, rummaging through her things looking for the charger to the iPad. Without over-thinking, I plugged the device in and left. Later in the day, once the iPad was charged, I sat back down at the desk and pulled back its grimy red cover. I placed my finger on the power button and there beneath the screen, frozen in time, found the girl I missed so much sitting behind a big ice cream sundae, smiling back at me from the picture she'd chosen as her screen saver. Her classic grin wide, her eyes sparkled, she was surrounded by friends.

I had opened Pandora's Box, and ready or not the memories came pouring out.

For years that iPad had been her constant companion.

"Plug it in by my bed, please."

"I'll text you if I need you in the night."

"I'll let you know when I wake up in the morning."

Her iPad helped her to communicate. She was particu-larly fond of making slideshows for people for any and all occasions.

"I need to work on the presentation I'm making Curt for his birthday."

"How do you spell Australia? Jason's there, I'm making him a slide show."

"Debbie had a long day at work, I'm working on some-thing to make her happy."

"Michelle and Mark are going on a trip, I made them a slide show about Florida."

"What hospital is Jessie going to have her baby at? I need to do some research for the special project I'm working on for her."

Whenever there was an anniversary or a birthday or a coming home or going away or a sporting event that someone she knew was interested in, or a cheering up or a congratulations needed, she was on it; slideshows were her specialty. Without fail, when Curt and I returned home from a trip, we'd find a ten-page slideshow (printed out) atop our bed pillows highlighting the city we visited, the hotel we stayed in, and photos of the exact planes and airports we'd flown. The slideshow was always tucked just behind the home-made welcome banner that we imagined she thought would be such a surprise to us, was something we counted on and adored. Her welcome-homes and the genuine effort she put into the details of those welcome-homes touched our hearts every time. Her welcome-homes, like all of her slideshows, illustrated her capacity for loving selflessly.

That little computer gave her purpose, and she was proficient on it. She searched for pictures of anything she needed to add the personal touch she wanted when she sent out emails. She wouldn't stop until she found the building you worked in or the car you drove - not just any car either. Satisfaction would not be attained until she found the exact make and model (and hopefully color) that was yours. If she sent an email to someone who had a Golden Retriever, there wasn't a chance in hell that she'd send them a picture of a Husky. She was diligent in her searches and was so proud of her completed "work."

Opening her music files, I laughed out loud. The music stored on her iPad was random and indiscriminate. She listened to and sang along with songs her choir class was singing, like, "Yes, We Have No Bananas," and" You Raise Me Up," and then she'd listen to hip-hop songs her brother would try to teach her. She listened to songs from Disney's *Frozen*, and to the pop chart songs her sister insisted were the best. She even liked the old school music we listened to. She knew which songs and sounds she liked best, *"Mom, will you download "God Bless America," "Jingle Bells," and that new Lumineers song for me?"* Her favorite band was a band called Dispatch though, and Dispatch was her favorite because the band's drummer was a friend of ours. Brad was good to her and made her feel special. He invited her to his concerts (huge sold-out events at Red Rocks) and let her sit on the stage; he made sure she always had his newest albums; he came to her hospital room when he was in town and played for her, much to the delight of all the young nurses. In the end, Brad played at her funeral. Her iPad was chock full of Dispatch songs.

When she sang, she sang loud and proud. She knew many of the lyrics to the songs she listened to, but like most of us, she misunderstood some of them, which caused her to sing the songs the way she heard them. Listening to her practice a song for choir class one evening, we heard clear as a bell that Joshua was fighting the battle of *"Cherry Coke, Cherry Coke, Cherry Coke."*

Scrolling through the pictures she stored on that iPad, I came across several pictures of our dog in various stages of annoyance —created, no doubt, by her thrusting the camera in his face to get just the right angle. I saw shots that showed half of his face, or just his paw, or maybe a close up of his eye. I came across candid photos of our grandson, and pictures of the food she was going to eat. Her food pictures, unlike most young people her age who took pictures of their food, weren't Instagram worthy. Hers were shots of instant oatmeal or her favorite— Hot Pockets. Like her style in music, she knew what she liked and didn't care what anyone thought.

That beloved little device allowed her to connect, to participate, to explore, to listen, to watch, and to share. She learned to use it insanely well, and it kept her busy when we weren't available. Her iPad made her feel a part of things. How grateful we were for its presence in her life, and how grateful I was to be able to sit at her desk and hang out with her again.

I clicked the little green message icon to open her texts. The messages and texts she sent were prolific. She sent good morning texts and good night texts: she sent well wishes and messages to tell us that she was praying for us. She let us know when she saw a helicopter or a fire truck. More than once she thought it necessary to tell us that the dog wanted to say hello, and she made sure to tell us she was going to work extra hard for us at whatever she was doing that day. She let us know that she was working on a surprise for one of us (which was never a surprise because she was always working on a surprise for someone) but gave us strict instructions not to tell. She let us know that she couldn't wait to see us. She wrote from her heart, she wrote what she was feeling, and rarely, if ever, wrote of the pain she was in. The last year of her life, there were many days where she didn't have enough strength to physically be part of the world that swirled outside of our home, or outside of the hospital she was captive in. The iPad gave her voice and gave her presence.

The voice she established through her messaging though, took some deciphering. Between her poor spelling and the computer's spell check, her texts sometimes were tricky and amusing to read. Instead of sounding words out, she read mostly by sight, so if a word looked like the word she was trying to spell, it was good enough. Reading her messages proves the theory that the mind is able to unscramble and make sense of words, as long as most of the letters are there, especially the first and the last.

The *"Good Moring"* text or email we'd receive each day was understandable. When she asked us to do something for her, she always asked nicely by adding the word *"pleasle."* Ever eager for us to figure out what she had to tell us, she asked us to *"gess."* She wrote to our friend Gary once to tell him she had a *"short toart"* which, upon consultation and confirmation, proved to be a sore throat.

Her misspellings were consistent. Each word that she misspelled she misspelled the same way each and every time, so in a way, she had developed her own little language. This language has been incorporated now into our family's everyday language so much so that I sometimes find myself forgetting what the proper spelling or pronunciation of a word is supposed to be. I've ordered *Benjamin waffles* for breakfast without even batting an eye, used the word, *underpits* instead of underarms, and have talked about the *street-come-cleaners* that come down our street in the spring long before realizing my mistake.

Looking through her iPad, I came across the message she sent out one day that went viral, well, viral through our small community of friends and family. The message was to our friend Deb, who she nicknamed Flicker because of the dumb fact that they flicked each other on the shoulder all the time. She sent a note to Deb to wish her a happy day and to tell her a little bit of news about what she would be doing that day. The email concluded with this outrageous autocorrect closing: *"Love you bunches, Fucker ~ your Little Fucker."*

Sitting there that day at the desk in the room that will forever be hers, I realized the perfect timing of my dad's desire for one of those screen-type-tablet-things that you tap with your finger. Two years later I was ready to look through those old memories and relive them with joy. Two years later it became clear to me just how fortunate I am. I have her written words, the pictures she took and music she loved, at my fingertips.

When I fold back the cover of her little red iPad, with just a tap of my finger, I can hang out with my girl on that little screen-type-tablet thing any time I choose.

14

Thirteen Years Old

A MONTH BEFORE Father's Day, when the TV news station she constantly watched asked kids to send letters explaining why "My Dad's the Best," she announced she was going to send a letter about Curt. She was thirteen. Curt and I had been married just a few years.

In an attempt to be sensitive to all parties concerned, I asked if she wanted to write the letter about her dad instead of her step-dad. But she was adamant. She wanted to write about Curt.

We sat down to write the letter. She dictated while I typed.

> *"My stepdad is the greatest to hang out with!*
>
> *I do lots of things with him that make us both happy- I wash the cars with him. I do the headlights, and the rear lights, and the tires, he does everything else.*
>
> *I go to the new office where he works—-I even helped him and everybody else move into it!*
>
> *I play basketball with my brother and with him, he*

is the best basketball player. He teaches me to dribble on the driveway.

My step-dad watches me at my Special Olympics swimming and cheers me on the loudest of everyone! He stands at the end of the pool with my towel. I swim fast to get down to where he is.

My stepdad teaches me how to do everything.

We go out for breakfast on Saturday mornings. We go out for breakfast just me and him, we let my mom sleep in. It's fun because he lets me eat so much more than my mom does! We get extra pancakes and sausage.

We eat ice cream every night and we stir it up until it's nice and mushy!

We work in the yard together and we take the dog on walks, and we work in the garage together. I have my own board to practice pounding nails into. I always make sure that he wears his safety goggles.

My stepdad takes me to the airport to look at planes, he helps me learn what each plane is called. He also takes me to the fire station to see the fire trucks and learn about them!

My stepdad takes such good care of me and my mom, and my brother and sister and our dog! He always watches out for me, and thinks about what would make us all happy.

I am very lucky to have him."

We sent the letter off and tried to forget about it, which wasn't easy because the letter was the first thing, and the only thing, she wanted to talk about every morning once Curt left for work.

I was in the far corner of the yard planting flowers, up to my elbows in dirt, the day she came out onto the back deck yelling that she'd won the contest. Not eager to get up from the mess I was working in, I hollered back, *"No you didn't, and I told you not to get your hopes up."* She yelled back stating firmly, that, YES, she'd won. *"C'mon,"* I shouted, *"How do you know?"* And that's when she walked up to me with her arm outstretched and the cordless phone in her hand telling me there was someone on the line who wanted to talk to me. That's the same moment it became clear to me that the person waiting on the other end of the phone had heard our entire conversation.

Trying my best to sound like a good mom, the kind of mom that would never yell across the yard to her kid, nor dash her child's most desired hopes and dreams, I wiped the dirt off my hands, put the phone to my ear, put a smile on my face, and in my best June Cleaver impression, said hello.

The person waiting to speak to me introduced herself as a reporter from the news station and readily accepted my apology for such a long delay in getting to the phone and for anything she may have heard while waiting. Then, with laughter in her voice, she told me that what my daughter had said was true; her essay had won, and Curt had been chosen "Best Dad." She told me that the station had received hundreds of essays from children describing their dads and that choosing just one had not been easy. She said that our letter stood out from the rest because of the simple and genuinely authentic way it described the love and admiration our girl had for her stepdad. What's more, she said, was the genuine way that this stepdad seemed to care for his entire family.

The reporter then began to discuss with me her thoughts on how the station wanted to give the award to Curt, who knew nothing about the contest or the essay that had been written about him. They wanted to surprise him with it live on the air in three days, so together we concocted a plan about meeting at a local park early on Friday morning to be part of a news story about Special Olympics.

While we gathered at the park, the letter would be read in the studio on the air. The reporter with us in the park would then conduct her interview with our girl and her step-dad where she'd explain to Curt that the Special Olympics story was just a ruse. She'd then bestow upon him the title of "Best Dad." As part of the award, the letter writer and her step-dad would receive box seats for six to an upcoming Rockies baseball game, and to top it all off (for our girl at least) the official mascot of the baseball team, Dinger the Dinosaur, would join us at the park to hand over the tickets.

Our girl was silly and goofy with excitement and anticipation, but miraculously kept the secret, or as she put it, she *"didn't drop the beans."*

Friday morning finally arrived, and because she knew she was going to be on television, she wore her favorite red T-shirt with the little white collar (she thought it kind of dressy). Because she knew she was to pretend like we were going to be talking about Special Olympics, she wore a couple of medals around her neck hanging of course, from red and green ribbons.

As requested by the reporter, our little family arrived at the park two days before Father's Day at 7:00 am. It was already warm and sunny and was going to be a perfect summer day. As we walked up to the park's pavilion, we were met by the camera crew, the reporter and Dinger the mascot, who spent the next several minutes hanging out with us, letting our girl get behind and in front of the camera, coaxing her to act like a reporter and speak into the microphone. She was a little shy with Dinger but held his hand.

Curt finally wondered out loud where the other families being interviewed were, and that's when the story went live. The reporter admitted to Curt that there was no Special Olympics interview happening and that the real reason he was at the park was because of a particular letter they had received from a certain someone he knew well, which told them just why her step-dad should be named "Best Dad."

Everything happened so quickly. Curt was surprised and humble, saying on air, what we all knew to be true - that he didn't feel that anything he did was extraordinary. He talked about how easy it is for him to love and care for our family and especially our girl, who stood squished next to him as close as she possibly could with her arm tucked safely into the crook of his.

When it was all over, we dropped her eagerly off at school (she couldn't wait to tell her friends and teachers about the morning) then Curt and I met my dad, who had been watching the morning news from home, for breakfast and a debriefing. The morning had been somewhat overwhelming for Curt, who hadn't heard or seen the letter yet, as it was read on air in the studio before they cut to us live in the park.

While we sat at the orange Village Inn breakfast table, I read the letter out loud; then my dad, through tear-filled eyes, told us about watching the segment from home. He told us that while they read the letter, pictures that I'd sent into the station of Curt and our girl living life together appeared on the screen. He told us that the newscasters were teary-eyed too.

Between congratulatory phone calls that poured in (due to the fact that I'd asked everyone we knew to watch the morning news that day), we celebrated our way through breakfast. Strangers at the table next to us raised their orange juice glasses and toasted with us. Waitresses came by to shake Curt's hand and to tell him they'd seen him on TV.

We received notes and emails throughout the week from friends and family and incredibly, some from people we'd never met. Some of the notes were to Curt, some of the notes were to me, and some of the notes were to our sweet girl, who poured over them all, and then placed them along with pictures from the day in a scrapbook for Curt to keep on his desk. Each note touched on the genuine relationship the two of them shared, and the remarkable way their relationship was so genuine.

That small rectangular black photo album that's beginning to show signs of wear, still sits, off to the right a little, but well within arm's reach, on Curt's desk today.

15

Two Years After

THERE'S A PLACE I go now, a place I like to stop by two, maybe three times a month when it's not too cold outside. When it's cold out, I rarely go. In fact, I try hard to not even think about this place when it's cold outside. This place isn't good in the winter. This place really isn't that great when it's not winter either, yet I go and keep going back. It's huge and easy to get to. This place is well maintained. Despite the fact that it is full of people, this place is quiet. Short visits have no admission fees. Long-term stays cost you everything. For now, my visits are short.

This place I go to is the cemetery. The stones I visit stand one in front of the other. My mother's name is engraved on the tall grey granite stone that stands in front; the small red stone polished smooth and shiny sits just behind it and to the right and bears the name of my daughter.

Growing up, a visit to Grama in her small Wyoming town usually meant a visit to the cemetery where her family was buried. My Gram went every week, out of duty or desire, I don't know. I never asked. Going to the cemetery was just a part of my grandmother's life. She went to the market, the cleaners, the library, and on her way home, of course, she'd stop at the cemetery. With no other choices offered, my brother and I were obliged to tag along.

Gravel crunched beneath our flat, rubber-tipped tennis shoes as we walked through the iron gates, and followed her to the site where her father's thin grey stone had been standing for over 40 years. We'd read along with her as she'd recite his name. She'd tell us stories of the sweet and tender father he was. She'd tell us how young both she and her father were when he died, she just fifteen, and her dad about 35; we'd get sad for her. And then she'd tell us how he died at home, and how his body remained in their living room for the next several days as people came by to pay their respects. She told us that she'd never forgotten how uncomfortable and strange that made her feel. I remember thinking how remarkable that sounded, that nobody died at home anymore and if they did, they didn't stick around inside the house long after they had expired. I remember thinking my Gram must be really old.

We walked slowly through the rows and rows of family and friends who used to inhabit the world outside this fenced-in space. We read the old names carved into each stone. My brother and I had our favorite, a guy named Delaney. We liked the way his smooth brown stone looked next to the open grassy expanse beside him. His dignified stone was the last one in the row along the fence. Each time we visited the cemetery, we'd check to see who had moved in near Delaney, and to whom the reigning title of "last one in" had been bequeathed.

Of all the folks we visited in the cemetery, the people I remember the most from Gram's stories were the ones that got away too soon, the people she hadn't gotten to love long enough. Those were the stories that broke my heart; those were the stories we coaxed her to tell over and over again. The story of the baby cousin who died of typhoid fever, and that baby's mother, who died in childbirth. The story of that baby's father, who died of a broken heart just a few months later. We listened to the story of Gram's eccentric, fun-loving sister who died in the prime of her life, and of course the story of their father who never got to see his daughters grow up.

Because our extended family was large and close, we were no strangers to death. Death visited on occasion, but nobody young had ever died on our watch. For my brother and I that made death seem sad but okay, a part of life. To us, death only happened a long time ago, or just to old people. Gram assured us that kids didn't die young anymore. She told us how fortunate we were to live in the time of penicillin, with its power to wipe out infection, and how fortunate we were to live during a time when diseases could be cured. She assured us that parents didn't die any more either, not at least until their children had grown old themselves. She told us that *"they grew them stronger than they used to,"* and we believed her. Our cemetery visits were never scary to me; they were glimpses into the past. They were interesting and oddly enough, sort of fun.

Trips to the cemetery were always with Gram. It never occurred to me to visit the cemetery without her. I did it because she did it. I did it because it was important to her, and she was important to me. I never observed her gleaning anything extra special from our trips to the cemetery; I never observed her in prayer there, or even in conversation with those she had lost. I remember watching her slide her fingers across the engraved names of her mother and father, and I remember her pulling the weeds that grew into crevices and cracks near the base of the stones. As she grew older, I remember her asking me if I thought I'd come to the cemetery when she was gone. I told her that of course, I would, even though I didn't believe for a second that I actually would.

Today, listening to the gravel crunch beneath my flat, rubber-tipped tennis shoes as I walk through the iron gates, Gram isn't with me. She's been gone for a year now. Her stone stands 100 miles away; she is buried next to my grandfather and near her parents in the cemetery of my youth. My mom has been gone for 20 years, and I yearn for her still. My sweet daughter has been gone for two. The cemetery I walk through today is the cemetery of my now, and the cemetery of my future. I'm here today because I want to be - not out of obligation or because someone has asked me to come. Gram would be happy.

I walk toward the two stones that stand one in front of the other - the grey one (my mom's) looks protective and wise, and the red one just behind it (that bears the name of my daughter) looks playful and bright. Armed with my bucket, my gloves, and my garden tools, I've become the groundskeeper for a few square feet of earth that has become precious to me. I delight with the bulbs and flowers that appear in the spring. I tend to them, add to them, thin them, water them, feed them, and protect them throughout the year. I pull the grass and weeds that grow in the cement crevices, just like Gram used to, and discover that I've found a place to be quiet, a place to remember, and if I want to, even a place to talk out loud to these women I miss. I think I've found what Gram may have felt as she wandered the rows of her cemetery — a sense of usefulness. Tending to the flowers has allowed me to dote on my mom, and it's given me a way to continue to take care of my girl. I've found something tangible to do for them that has an assuaging effect on my grief.

Now it's my grandson who tags along with me through rows and rows of stones. At four years old I know only one sure thing about our trips together to the cemetery: I know that he has fun there. He likes helping me water and weed and prune. He likes to help me take care of his auntie, and when he gets bored, he likes to hide behind the big stones. For now, at least, he likes to listen to short stories about how much his auntie loved him, and he likes to listen to me talk about my mother.

Years from now I'll stand in the cemetery next to this grandson grown taller than me. I'll rub my fingers across the precious names engraved into the stones and ask him if he thinks he'll come to the cemetery and walk the rows after I'm gone.

16

Thirteen to Eighteen Years Old

BEING A PART of things was a big part of who she was. She liked being involved, and she liked being included. She (like most of us) desired to be part of groups. But she (unlike most of us) had no fear acting on that desire. If there was a club looking for new members, she was their girl; ready to join.

It's not that she craved friendships, or that she despised being alone, she simply saw no reason not to be a part of things. She didn't consider (like the rest of us) whether or not she'd like the other people in the group; she just would. And she didn't consider (like the rest of us) whether or not the other people in the group would like her; she simply trusted they would. She didn't give much consideration to whether she'd be any good at the club's activity; she'd merely try her best. Nor did she consider the possible judgment that may come her way due to her ability or lack thereof; she saw no reason to judge. When she heard of an opportunity to be a part of something fun, she wanted in.

The problem was that not all clubs would have her, and not all clubs were for her. We helped her look for groups where she'd have a chance at success. She was ready, willing and open to suggestions.

When she was five, she started dance class at the neighborhood dance studio where her big sister danced a few times a week. She was comfortable in the studio because of the hours she'd spent there watching Jessie dance; it didn't hurt either, that my aunt owned the studio. She was welcomed to dance class with open arms and showed up each week in her pretty pink leotard and ballet shoes. She loved it.

She had rhythm and could keep a beat. It didn't matter to her (or she didn't notice) that she was always a second or two behind the other girls in the class as they moved to the music. And it didn't bother her (or she didn't notice) that when she leapt across the dance floor, her feet never left the ground. She paid no attention to the fact that her pliés and relevés weren't as high or as low as the other little ballerinas in her class. She proudly danced her heart out every week and cherished being part of the class.

In 2nd grade, she joined a Brownie Troop. Meetings were held Wednesday afternoons right after school. Wednesday quickly became her favorite day of the week. Wednesday not only meant fun after school, Wednesday meant she'd get to wear her beloved Brownie uniform the entire day. To her, that drab brown uniform was a badge of honor, which announced to the world that she was part of something great.

The other girls in the troop were good to her and the leaders kind. She took part in all the craft making, the song singing, the outdoor activities, and the good deed doing. We worked hard with her at home teaching her how to hold three fingers in the air and how to recite the Brownie Pledge. We cried the day she stood up in front of the Brownie Troop stating that, on her honor, she'd do her best, to serve God and her country, to help people, and that she'd live by the Girl Scout Law.

Her favorite part of being a Brownie by far was the cookie selling part. Cold calls did not intimidate her. Our kitchen counter became her call center. She was prepared to contact everyone she'd ever met to ask for their support. I sat by her side and played secretary helping her when it became hard for the person on the other end of the line to understand her. I wrote down all the names and addresses of her customers, but she made all the calls herself. She sold box after box of cookies. She was a superstar cookie seller and proud to be part of a club.

In 3rd grade, she was asked to play on a basketball team with some neighborhood friends. I was beside myself with Happy that she was asked, and concerned about the reality of how it would go. She could barely run and most definitely didn't have the strength or skills to shoot a basket. How would the kids treat her, would they understand? Would they be nice? Would the parents understand, would they be nice? Would she get hurt? None of this concerned her or crossed her mind. She wanted to play. We let her.

She played with the girls for two years. They were appropriately kind to her. They didn't baby or coddle her; they gave her opportunities to dribble and pass the ball as best she could. She became the team's official in-bounder and was very happy with her position through the 5th grade when it was made clear to us, by one of the team moms, that our girl's basketball career with this team at least, would be over at the end of the season. I was told that the other girls on the team were maturing and were ready for more, (*"wait, my girl is maturing too,"* I didn't say) and then I was told winning had become something that now mattered.

I almost understood (and even felt sorry for) the mom who had to give me the bad news. She was decent enough, and she actually didn't use the words I heard her saying, that my girl was just taking up space, but I felt it, and I will never forget how painful it was to have the rug pulled out from under me. Naively, I hadn't expected this to happen. Naively, I became content and complacent. I should have seen it coming; I should have been more aware. It would have hurt less. Lesson learned.

We filled the void with Special Olympics, and she didn't miss a beat. We told her that in middle school it was common for kids to join new teams. She joined a soccer team in the fall and a basketball team in the winter. She was hooked. She bowled and swam year round. She went to dances and parties with her friends from Special Olympics and was thrilled to belong.

She joined school choirs because she liked to sing; she didn't have a great voice, but her enthusiasm usually made up for it. The choir teachers were always happy to have her, until her junior year of high school that is, when a new music teacher was hired.

Curt and I would miss the Christmas concert because we were going to be out of town. Instead, we attended the dress rehearsal of the performance. We sat in the darkened audience of the high school auditorium and spotted our girl right where she'd told us to look; top riser, right side, next to her buddy Matt. They were easy to spot because they were the only ones wearing Santa hats. The two of them stood side by side singing loudly and happily. They followed the new choir teacher's directions. They smiled and clapped their hands and bobbed their heads along with the rest of the kids when they were supposed to. They were singing Christmas carols and thoroughly enjoying themselves.

This was not an elite school choir. This was a choir that was open to anyone who wanted to join, so, of course, our girl had joined. This choir was not world class, but they weren't terrible either. They were fun to watch. While we sat in the school auditorium, we watched as the new music teacher abruptly stopped the rehearsal and asked our girl and her friend Matt not to sing. We watched as she asked them not to clap their hands or bob their heads because their timing was off. We watched as their faces fell. Curt held me down in my seat for the next agonizing minute or two until the rehearsal came to a close.

The kids filed off the stage, and I filed myself up to the new teacher. Fortunately, for her sake, the head of the music department (a man I knew well) cut me off at the pass and asked me to allow him the opportunity to handle the situation.

The apology I received later that day from the new teacher asking forgiveness for her inexcusable behavior did little to erase the way I felt about her or would continue to feel. The apology she gave my girl and her buddy Matt, however, was received quite differently. They immediately forgave her. They continued to sing in the choir, and they never gave it a second thought. Much to my chagrin and amazement, the new choir teacher became one of their all-time favorite teachers.

In middle school, she joined a cheerleading team. Apparently, while I wasn't looking, cheerleading had become a sport that was taught and practiced at gyms around the country. A gym (not close to our house) was one of those gyms and was offering a cheerleading program for kids of all abilities. The program director had a young daughter with special needs and was passionate about giving kids with disabilities a chance at this growing sport. Practice, she said, would not be optional. She stressed the fact that along with having fun, the participants would have to take the team seriously. The program director said that joining the team was a commitment and that she was willing to take any kid who would make that commitment. My girl, of course, was ready to sign on the dotted line immediately; she had absolutely no problem with commitment - in fact, she thrived on it. The commitment problem was mine - committing meant a drive across town in rush hour at least once a week. We committed and made that drive every week until high school graduation.

The cheerleading team was perfect for her: she had somewhere to be every week— *("they are counting on me")*— she knew everyone at the gym — *("they know me")* — she owned a uniform she was able to wear every week, she tried and mastered new skills, which gave her confidence and an increased sense of balance, but mostly she made friends that she adored.

Cheerleading was, as it turns out, a serious sport. Through the years, we attended competitions where thousands of girls competed to win prizes and trophies. We saw hard work, perfection, lots of smiles and lots of dramatic tears. Our girls were given a place of honor at these competitions. They were asked to perform, not to compete. When our girls took center stage with spotlights shining, large arenas went quiet. When the music began, and our girls started their routine, they quickly became an inspiration. They were good! Their hard work was obvious.

They danced, and they jumped, they did stunts, and they smiled. By the end of their performances, there were no dry eyes in the house. The cheers from the audience were over-whelming. Our girls were proud to be out there. Our girls were proud of each other and their team as a whole. The pep talks they gave were authentic, and were delivered from the heart, *"Let's get out there and do our best, because we are the best, right?"* they'd assure each other. *"Don't be afraid; I've got your back, okay."* Learning from their coaches and the athletes around them, they took their cheerleading seriously.

We traveled with these girls to various arenas around town, and we traveled with them to Disney World a few times where they performed at national cheerleading competitions. They were a motley crew, these girls of all types, some long and lean, others less so. Some of the girls were able to jump and do cartwheels, some barely able to lift a foot off the ground. Some wore wheelchairs, and some wore braces. They all wore the sparkly silver bow of their cheerleading uniform atop their heads.

Collectively, they were empowered and a joy to watch. The confidence they exuded as a team was a tribute to who each of them was as an individual.

Sometimes, watching her in a group, I'd feel a lump form in my throat and a sob on its way to escaping my lips. I was so proud of her, I was so happy for her, and if I'm perfectly hon-est, I was sometimes sad for her when I thought about what her life might have been had she been born disability-free. But that was my Sad, not hers, and it didn't come very often. She loved the life she had, and I loved watching the way she lived it.

17

Fifteen Years Old

SHE LOVED THE color red. The red clothes that hung in her closet, and the red clothes that were folded in her drawers, were the clothes she preferred to wear. Around her wrist, she wore a watch with a huge face and a wide red leather band. Year after year, the backpack she chose to carry was, you guessed it, red. A friend made her a pair of red earrings for her birthday once, and that was that, we never had to purchase another pair of earrings again. The little red flowers adorned her ears every day. The frames of her eyeglasses were red, and she always chose the shiniest brightest red polish the nail shop near our house had to offer. She was sure that her extra wide, extra flat, size 12 feet, and her big puffy hands looked best when her nails were polished red. Her hands were distinct and unforgettable. They were strong hands, and we could feel their strength when she squeezed ours tightly when she held them. But those hands lacked tone and were squishy (the word Jessie used to describe them aptly) when her hands were at rest. The red polish she wore spoke volumes about her confidence. She truly loved being who she was.

During her high school years, we discovered Special Olympic Swimming. She was healthy for the most part in high school. She had strength and stamina then, and swimming turned out to be a great sport for her. She wasn't an elegant swimmer, and she wasn't fast, but she could hold her own and make it down a lane and back in the pool. She loved being part of the team. She felt like what she was doing was important, and she worked hard never to let her teammates down. "I can do it," she'd say, "they are counting on me". Our girl wasn't competitive, but she was happy when she improved her time, and the coach offered her praise.

Saturday mornings were devoted, in the winter months, to swim practice. We'd arrive at the school parking lot, bundled in coats and hats, with the other families. Some parents were able to drop their high school athletes off at the curb knowing their child would be able to walk over ice and snow carrying their overstuffed swim bag and successfully make it to the locker room without slipping on the wet floor. They knew their child could change into a swimsuit without help. Some of the kids were able to adjust their own goggles and pull back their hair on their own. Some of these athletes were able to get into the pool on their own. But our swimmer, even at her best, needed our assistance, so it was up to me to accompany her into the locker room each week and help her change into her swimsuit. I wasn't the only mother in the locker room; there were a few of us there doing what needed to be done to help our teenage daughters in and out of their clothes. We tried to act like what we were doing was normal and fun; we knew better than to dwell on the monotony of our responsibility, or to think about how long we'd be doing things like this. Our girls were part of something great - the teamwork, the friendships, the competition, the exercise. It was fun for our girls;

therefore, it was fun for us. Except sometimes when it stung, those times I'd let myself stop long enough to think about the fact that we were in a high school locker room helping our high school daughters with their high school bodies in and out of swimsuits like we'd done when they were pre-schoolers. It stung to know that we'd probably be helping them change in and out of clothes for the rest of our lives. Consequently, I usually didn't allow myself to stop long enough to think about those things. I knew that it was best for me, best for us all really, to laugh and joke and smile and stay positive with the task at hand —no matter how long it took to shimmy in and out of a wet bathing suit. Each week I practiced patience in that locker room.

Meet days were LONG, really long. Getting out of a meet in less than six hours made us feel like we'd won the lottery. Meet days, we'd claim a corner of the indoor pool area to call our own and hunker down with our lawn chairs, blankets, snacks, lunch and things to read.

Curt and I had a routine each time she was up to swim. Curt would stand ready with her towel on the side of the pool where the race would end. I'd position myself on the opposite side of the pool (the starting side) and crouch low behind her on the pool deck, talking to her while she waited in the water (because she was unable to dive off the block) for the whistle to blow. Curt and I would stand there on our respective sides and watch her hands and feet slam through the water in what was supposed to be a freestyle lap, then watch as she'd switch to breast style when she became fatigued. We'd watch her bob up for a big gulp of air, and because there wasn't a pair of goggles anywhere on earth made large enough to fit the circumference of her head, we'd see that her goggles were half filled with water. We'd encourage her with whoops and hollers until she'd made it and reached the end. Strong Curt would extend his arm down to her and somehow get her wet, heavy body out of the pool while he discreetly covered her with a towel to successfully avoid exposure due to inevitable wardrobe malfunctions.

The medal ceremonies were the best. They were orchestrated just as they are in the Olympics, with the gold medal winner standing on a platform a little higher than the silver and bronze medal winners. At swim meets we'd watch athletes of all shapes and sizes stand, wrapped in their beach towels, on these platforms ready to receive their medals. Their hair dripped into puddles beneath them as their names were announced and medals were placed around their necks. It seemed that their faces weren't big enough to hold their smiles —their parents' faces weren't either. The support the athletes had for each other, whether in consolation or congratulations, was genuine. High fives, hugs, and hurrahs were everywhere.

The day she swam her best came after she'd been swimming with Special Olympics for about two years. She was a sophomore in high school when she came in first place for the 50 freestyle. She stood atop the uppermost platform, holding hands with a friend of hers, who came in second place and stood a level below. I watched through tear-filled eyes and heard her name announced through cheers and applause. The gold medal was placed around her neck. Looking down to admire it, she discovered that the gold medal was hanging from a blue ribbon. Her smile disappeared.

When she showed Curt and me the medal she'd won, all she could talk about was the crummy blue ribbon it hung from. To her, it made absolutely no difference that the medal was gold, or that blue signified the best. Her voice began to waiver and then she told us that what she wanted was a red ribbon. We explained to her that blue meant that she'd won it all, that blue meant that she was the fastest. We told her that the red ribbon was good too, but that red was reserved for second place winners. We told her that blue was the ribbon that everyone hoped to receive.

But clearly, blue was not the ribbon she was hoping for. If first place meant a blue ribbon and a gold medal, she'd rather have come in second place with its silver medal and coveted red ribbon. After some behind-the-scenes explanations with scorekeepers and judges, the blue ribbon was traded in for red, and a second medal ceremony took place. Her friends again high-fived and hugged her, this time admiring the gold medal that hung from the red ribbon around her neck.

The world was made right again; the smile reappeared on her face.

18

Sixteen Years Old

SHE WAS NEVER going to be able to obtain a driver's license, that one seemed for sure. We still held out hope for many other milestones of maturity, but driving wasn't one of them; her reaction times weren't fast enough for one thing. Allowing her to drive unassisted would have been dangerous, for her and every other driver on the road. We never talked with her about it, this fact that she couldn't get her license. It was just one of those things that she knew and accepted without disappointment or worry.

When we taught her brother and sister how to drive, she appointed herself chief navigator and assistant driving instructor. She'd take her place in the back seat of the car and shout out instructions regarding things like speed, and just where the next turn would be. She mostly offered praises to the driver, and her laughs and giggles calmed the nerves of both student and teacher.

She never asked when it would be her turn to learn to drive.

Once each of the older kids obtained their license, they

quickly became her preferred chauffeur. Driving in their cars, she learned lyrics and actions to rap music and that drive-thru restaurants have happy hours. Driving in their cars, she was cool, and she knew it.

Ever the rule follower refusing to take the wheel when any of us asked her to (and we asked her to plenty) I was shocked the warm Sunday afternoon she agreed to give it a try. I'd driven her to an empty parking lot of a nearby office building. Being fairly certain this driving thing was more for me than for her, I was prepared. I bribed her with candy, ice cream, money... whatever it took until she finally gave in and traded seats with me. It was then that I began to realize that I hadn't thought my plan all the way through. She looked completely adorable sitting there in the driver's seat of my little black convertible with its top down, but what would happen next? It was then that I realized that there were at least two critical things that I hadn't considered: number one - there was (what felt like a mountain between us) the gear shifter, the parking brake and the console, and number two - she didn't know anything about the foot pedals, including which one made the car go and which one made the car stop.

Afraid to lose momentum or her willingness to drive, I pushed myself up onto the console and flung my left leg over to the driver's side, which made my head stick out above the windshield, but— gave me access to the pedals. I planted my other leg firmly onto the passenger seat for stability. We were ready to roll.

Next, we had a discussion of where her hands should be placed upon the wheel. She told me that she remembered what we had taught her brother and sister. She told me that her hands should be placed at *12:00* and *4:00*, which was close enough to the actual 10:00 and 2:00, and was good enough for me; so we went with it.

I asked her to turn the key and start the car. We moved so slowly at first, it felt as if we weren't moving at all. We gained speed as we gained confidence and we rode around and around that parking lot for over an hour.

She assumed her role as navigator, and with her hands on the wheel, she led us in the direction she wanted to go. My role was to move us forward or back and to figure out when to accelerate or when to slow us down. These were the roles I longed for in our everyday. I was hopeful that the day would come when she'd be one to decide the direction her life would take and was desirous of the possibility to help her arrive there safely.

She completely indulged me in our slow drive across the parking lot in one direction, then our slow journey back the other. She obliged my occasional request for a circle or a left turn for some extra excitement but it was obvious, of the two of us, I was the one having the most fun. She liked it enough but was ready to call it quits at any time.

When we decided to stop and send a picture of her to the rest of the family, we were interrupted by a policeman who appeared out of nowhere. He stood next to the driver's side door and asked the now-panicked student driver if she had her driver's permit. While she sat there and stared at him with her hands firmly planted at 12:00 and 4:00, I climbed off the console bringing my head back into the car, then eased myself back into the passenger seat. Trying desperately to be discrete, I swung my left leg back over to its rightful position. I straightened my windblown hair, held my girl's hand and explained to the nice officer what was going on, then held my breath this story would end in a positive way. He told us he'd received a call from someone in the office building asking him to come and check things out.

He was a nice guy, but our driving lesson was over.

The police officer watched as we traded places once again; me back in the driver's seat calling all the shots, my girl the happy passenger, now free to wave goodbye as we drove out of the parking lot.

My heart danced that day — the day she sort of drove. I laughed out loud at just how cute she'd been behind the wheel, and found joy in how fun and sort of normal this coming of age ritual had been. Her joy though, grew bigger and louder, and prouder each and every time she retold the story — the story about the day that "my mom got us in so much trouble that someone called the cops".

19

One Year Later

THERE'S SAD AROUND me today. It's been hanging around for a few weeks now. I'm not very good at paying attention to Sad. In fact, I have become quite the expert at avoiding it. Okay, so maybe not avoiding it completely... but I'd say that Sad is something I'm learning to ignore.

When Sad comes, I usually say hello to it (like Seinfeld used to say hello to Newman, with unhidden disdain.) Sometimes I'll even shake its hand and then hurry away without finding out how Sad is doing or what it wants. I don't give Sad much time, because I suppose I don't want Sad to give me much time. Sad is a drag, and Sad takes too long. While I know that Sad can be productive, I just don't want to sit with Sad all that much anymore. I've sat with Sad quite a bit. I've become weary of Sad.

Today though, Sad is clinging to me and won't let go. My best efforts to shake free are falling short. My usual distractions just aren't working.

The music I'm blaring through the house today (usually a sure fire way to pick up my mood) includes all my favorites; yet the only songs I really hear are the sad songs, the songs that remind me of life Before — like Carol King's, "Child of Mine" (the song that I used to joyfully sing to each of my young children), or life During - like Natalie Merchant's, "Wonder" (the song I used to listen to with hope as she sang about a child who'd not suffer), or life right After - like Laura Story's, "Blessings" (that encouraged me to believe that healing might come through tears).

Baking my family's favorite oatmeal chocolate chip cookies, the ones I've baked for years, another reliable mood fixer, fell short today as well, as tears ran down my cheeks and into the batter.

Deciding it would be good for me to sit down and write, the room I was drawn to was the room that used to be hers — the room I don't go into much anymore except to put something away or to look for a particular item. I don't dwell in that room, but today I can't pull myself away.

Leaning my head back on the sofa as I sing along with one of her favorites, "Ain't No Valley High Enough (a song she liked because it was in the movie Step Mom, not because she was a big Diana Ross fan or even knew who Diana Ross was) I notice four pieces of scotch tape stuck to the ceiling. It occurs to me then that the comfy spot on the old family room sofa that now inhabits this room where I sit is placed just where her bed used to be, and the tape that's left on the ceiling once held four pretty little cut-out paper hearts that I made for her.

Gazing at the ceiling at that leftover tape, through eyes filled with tears, I vividly imagine those pink and purple and white three-dimensional hearts, each hanging at different lengths from pieces of thin, twisted, red thread.

This is the spot she laid her head too.

This is what she saw in the morning when she woke up, in the evening when she went to sleep, and in the end, this is what she looked at when she lay in bed throughout the day because she was too weak to get up.

> All the times she must have looked up at those hearts!
>
> All the times she waited for me to come to her room.
>
> All the times she texted me saying, "no joke mom I need you."
>
> All the times I could have moved a bit faster, put aside what I was doing a little bit quicker........ All the times I could have spent a minute more with her.

When she looked at those hearts, did she know how much I loved her? I absolutely know that she knew — even though I absolutely know that she never thought of things like that.

Love in her life was a given, she gave it so well, and she received it without question.

She was blessed with an innocence that suited her.

Worry was something that she did not know.

She received love from us and from everyone around her.

Love was the way it worked.

She didn't know otherwise.

And I don't believe she ever gave it a second thought.

She never had to think about love, or being cared for, she just always was......loved and cared for. I'm content that's the way we did it. I'm thankful that we could, but mostly I'm forever grateful that she never had to think about it - not once, not ever.

20 | Fifteen to Eighteen Years Old

SHE WAS DONE with middle school and would attend our neighborhood high school along with three thousand, nine hundred and ninety-nine other students. We hyped it up, of course, just like we'd done with our other kids the summer after they completed middle school, but this time we weren't able to hype it with such confident enthusiasm. We didn't exactly know how high school would play out for this third child of ours, or if anything we'd say would be true for her...... We hyped it up nonetheless.

"You made it; you get to go to high school!" "It'll be great." "You'll love it." "There's so much to look forward to: the football games, the clubs, the classes, and better lunches. You can even go off campus for lunch." "You're going to meet so many new kids." "You're going to make so many new friends."

The things we went on about, the things that were supposed to be good, and exciting and new, were the very things that kept me up each night that summer before she started high school.

Football games. How would that work? Would we have to go with her, would she stick out as the girl who had to go to the football game with her parents? Maybe she'd be invited to go to games with typical students— that would be great, but how would that work? Would they walk slowly enough for her to keep up? Would they help her navigate the steps of the stadium? Would they stay with her and include her once they got to the game?

Clubs. Would there be clubs she could join? Drama— probably not drama. Debate Team— definitely not Debate Team. Track Team—no. Art Club— maybe, but what would the other kids in the club say about the elementary art she would produce?

Classes in high school were hard. How in the world was she going to get anything out of the classes she would attend? Would she be isolated or segregated in a classroom that wouldn't challenge her? Or would she sit in classrooms where the material presented was over her head? Would it be possible for her to continue learning at a pace and level appropriate to her needs? Would there be a way for her to meet and mingle with the "regular kids?" And would those "regular kids" be nice to her?

Better lunches. I knew that lunches at the high school meant going off campus, and for freshmen who couldn't drive yet, that meant walking to the few restaurants near the school. Would she be able to walk that far? Would she be included in lunch outings? How would she handle paying for her lunch without understanding the value of money? Would she end up being stuck at school eating alone in the cafeteria?

And friends..... would she make new friends?

I'd conjured up so many images of what high school might be for her; the best case scenario was the one where she was embraced by the entire student body, the one where she attended all regular education classes, and the one where she became homecoming queen. Worst case scenario was the one where she spent her entire day bullied and alone.

The reality was neither.

The reality was she spent most of her school day in just one of the many buildings on campus, and for that matter in just one wing of that building, moving between only two classrooms. She spent the majority of her time at school tucked safely away in the building that held the Special Education Department, where students were grouped (as could best be determined) in classes based upon social and academic abilities. The spectrum was vast, but for the most part, my girl was with kids she was similar to and with kids to whom she could relate. Despite our concerns that she be pigeonholed or labeled, we would come to find out that being grouped with peers in the Special Education wing of the High School was the best and right place for our girl to learn and to grow and to be.

Her freshman year, she came home day after day telling us about a boy she had met named Mac. She was crazy about Mac. Mac was a senior, and she thought he was the coolest guy in the school. Apparently, she hung out with Mac a lot. She told us he made her laugh all the time and he was so nice. She wanted to invite Mac over. I went with her into school one day to meet this Mac fellow. She excitedly marched me up to meet a handsome boy, sitting in a wheelchair who could neither shake my hand in greeting nor say hello. Mac was non-verbal. He smiled with his eyes, and he melted her heart.

The kids she hung out with took friendship seriously. They didn't judge, "So you can't talk very well? That's okay; we'll be patient with you — you can be our friend." "So, you can't walk? No problem, we can push your wheelchair." "You sometimes act out? We don't mind, we'll give you a second chance, and a third chance and a fourth." Oh, they had their drama, which was fun to listen to on the way home in the car sometimes, "*Susie flipped me off again today.*" (Susie was the girl who flipped everyone off all the time. I'm fairly certain none of them knew exactly what that meant, including Susie.) "*Emily keeps calling Robert on the phone, and she wore fancy shoes to school today.*" (Emily was the girl who dressed pretty provocatively and who had a crush on a different boy every week.) "*Grant is sick today; we should find out what's the matter and make him a card.*" It was mostly innocent drama, and how sweet it was for them to support each other, and to figure things out.

This group of oddball kids, who didn't walk or talk or look like the rest of the student body so much, with their wheelchairs and walkers and unsteady gates, whose voices were probably louder than they should have been, and whose enthusiasm for the day was always expressed far more boisterously than their "typical" peers, who so desperately tried to play it cool, stuck together.

Groups become groups because of commonalities. This unique group of kids became friends because they had shared experiences with doctors and therapists, and frequent visits to the nurse's office, and daily medications. This group of kids became friends because they knew what not being the fastest kid in the gym class felt like, and they became friends because they knew that sometimes getting your point across takes more than one try. These kids, for the most part, shared values. Most importantly they shared the value of not caring what a person looked like or how they acted. These kids formed a high school group, and they belonged — not unlike the jocks, the nerds, the druggies or the cheerleaders.

I'm not sure what the rest of the student body referred to the group as, but I do know that they gladly referred to themselves as the Special Ed Kids, and to them, there was absolutely nothing wrong with the moniker.

She did interact with the rest of the student body when she attended electives like gym class, art class or choir; classes she liked very much. What she especially enjoyed though, and talked about almost every day, was the fun she had walking down the halls with her Special Ed friends on their way to her electives.

The Special Ed Kids did attend football games together. Sometimes we went with them, and sometimes they went on their own. The kids had parties together too- high school parties without beer, without pot, without sex. They had parties parents were invited to attend (at least for a little while), and they had parties where they played games and danced and laughed.

High school was where we began to think about her future with more clarity. High school was where we spent hours with counselors and teachers discussing who our girl was and how she learned. It was high school where we verbally expressed our acceptance of specific facts, like math wasn't her strong suit, and that she'd never understand money, and that a debit card could help her bypass that issue as long as we kept track of it for her.

Our girl had no need for a biology class that taught her the breakdown of a cell, or a geography class that taught her the terrain of Asia, especially when there were other classes to learn about animals she could see at the zoo or the map of the US she loved so much. Reading and writing were skills she needed for independence, so she attended classes that taught the type of reading she could comprehend, and writing skills (like learning how to make lists and leave notes for family and friends) that would be of value.

The classes she took in high school taught grocery shopping, and housekeeping, and how to use public transportation. Her classes focused on things that mattered to her, interested her, and would be of use to her. She learned about weather and current events, and how to safely navigate the internet. Each week she had the opportunity to experience some type of practical on-the-job training the school set up with local businesses around town. Some days she worked in her favorite Mexican restaurant where she helped set tables; some days she worked at a pizza place, folding boxes and organizing supplies. She helped out at a senior day-care facility serving lunches, and she worked in the office of a Catholic church where she helped collate and file papers.

She was productive in school and was happy learning things that were worthwhile. She took a class that taught her to shop for groceries independently that included a weekly visit to the market. Soon she learned and became familiar with the store and knew just where to find the items she wanted or needed or to ask for help when necessary. She also learned the protocol (that most of us take for granted, but there are nuanced rules) on how to check out and how to pay when her grocery shopping was complete.

Having learned all of this, shopping for our family became

a highlight of her week. It thrilled her (and I have to admit, thrilled me a little too) when she'd escort us into the coffee shop at the grocery store, take the list we'd made together at home and tell us to "sit back, relax and enjoy the show", which was her way of indicating that we were to stay where we were, she'd take care of the shopping. Thirty minutes later (it would have taken me at least an hour) she'd return with a smile and a full shopping cart, never missing even a single item.

She was proud to show us the correct way to set and clear the table, and her days doing office work made her feel important. Our girl gained both ability and confidence in high school; her Special Ed classes were practical, useful and empowering.

Her high school years revealed to us a fact that we knew to be true but were reticent to admit, a fact that, with our older two kids, we never even questioned. Her entire life, we'd made it our mission to make sure she was included. We taught her that she was terrific and smart and could do or be a part of anything she set her mind to, which served her well. She was confident and assured. Her entire life, we'd made it our mission to demonstrate and bring awareness to the community around us that people with disabilities and differences were less different than they appeared, which I believed, served our community well too. Our disconnect came in the subtle manner that we discounted (to some degree) she was happiest being with friends that were like-minded, and she was most productive in situations that stretched her but were within her realm of understanding and capability. Our efforts to include her in the larger community and teach her to be and hang out with the majority perhaps denied her (in some way) the possibility of shining in the glory of who she really was.

She gained maturity those high school years, and ultimately so did we. When we imagined her adult life (the life that seemed so far away but knew would eventually come), we 'd always imagined it with a healthy mix of hope and fear.

Because we'd seen some real possibilities, both social and practical through her surprisingly positive high school experience, we slowly and maybe even eagerly began to reach forward to that future fast on its way.

21

Seventeen Years Old

SHE WENT TO her high school prom when she was a junior. She had a date - her friend David, who was a year ahead of her in school. David lived up the street; they'd known each other since elementary school and had always been in the same special education classes. David was a cool kid; I'd never seen him without a smile on his face. He was itching to go to prom. He asked her if she'd go with him, and she said yes. David was outwardly excited about it, but she, as usual, took the invitation in stride and wasn't nearly as enthusiastic as her sister Jessie and I were.

We made a big fuss out of getting her a new dress. We took her sweet friend Amy along with us to pick it out. Amy's excitement matched Jessie's and mine, and Amy's enthusiasm was contagious. She and our girl squealed with joy each time we pulled a dress from the rack.

The four of us piled into a dressing room. Jessie, Amy and I each helping our girl in and out of dresses and giving opinions until the perfect black taffeta, sleeveless, V-neck dress with the pretty waistline and A-line skirt, was chosen. Jess and

I pushed hard for this choice, and felt strongly that we needed to be the voice of reason, as the two younger girls were getting their hearts set on a hot pink satin number with lots of ruffles and a very short skirt.

The laughter, along with all the oohs and the ahhs coming from our dressing room, had the immediate effect of clearing out every other dressing room around us. The looks I got each time I opened the dressing room door in search of another size or color made me smile. I didn't care what other people thought; I didn't care how loud the girls were. I was buying my girl a dress to go to her high school prom.

Plans for prom were underway. There would be three couples in this group of happy prom goers, all kids she'd known for years from Special Ed. The boys in the group were her favorites.

It was decided they'd go to prom, like most kids, in a limousine, which worked out perfectly since none of these kids had their driver's license.

The pictures, with all the parents gathered around like paparazzi, would be taken at our house. We'd known from years past (thanks to our older children) that the preferred prom picture was the one where all the kids were lined up with their dates on the stairs in cascading order from tallest to shortest. However, with this special group of kids, it was decided beforehand that the better option would be to take pictures on the flat ground in front of our fireplace, where there would be no possibility of anyone falling.

Once pictures were taken, they'd leave our house and head to a nice Italian restaurant, have dinner, go to the dance and then come home. Perfect. No after party, no drinking, no worries. Except these:

* How would she know what to order at the restaurant?
* Would she be able to clean her face well enough after dinner so that she wouldn't go to prom with spaghetti sauce lining her lips and spread onto her cheeks like blush?
* How would they pay for dinner? (None of them was very good with cash).
* How would they leave a tip?
* Would they make as much noise in the fancy restaurant as we had made in the dressing room when we picked out the dress?
* Would she get too tired? (She usually went to bed around 8:30).
* Would her feet hurt? (It was hard to find dress shoes that fit her feet. Should I send along flip-flops, and if I did, where would she carry them?)
* Would the limo driver be responsible? (Would he take advantage of them?)
* Would the other kids at the prom be kind?
* Would they dance?
* Would they have fun?

David's mom and I got to work. She arranged for dinner to be paid for on her credit card and arranged for the appropriate tip to be added by the manager, who would also look out for the kids while they were in his restaurant. He would be sure to give David's mom a call if anything seemed amiss, which was a much better plan than our original one of sitting at another table in the same restaurant while they ate, in case they needed us. The kids wouldn't have especially liked that, and we wouldn't have either except for the fact that we would have been allowed the pleasure of watching them navigate their way through the evening, all dressed up and acting like grown-ups.

We studied the menu with our kids before they went out so that they'd know what to ask for when it came time to order. Choosing was no problem for David; he knew he wanted some type of dressed-up chicken tenders, which made it easy for our girl, who decided to do the same. Hurray!, No messy sauce! Just in case, I packed her a little purse with a couple of wet wipes. I also planned to stash a small bag with flip-flops into the limo.

The day of the prom, Jessie came over, armed with a curling iron, hairpins, and makeup. She woke her sister from the nap I'd made her take. It was now time to get ready for the big night.

The two of them in the bathroom that afternoon had a blast. The younger sister sat on a chair at the vanity in her bra and underwear admiring herself in the mirror while the older sister stood behind her curling and primping and putting on the finishing touches. I don't know whose smile was larger. Through the music they had blasting, I heard Jessie talking to her about dancing. She was teasing her about slow dancing with David. The moans and groans and laughter coming from the bathroom between the two sisters that day were perfect, just as they should have been.

Doing a typical big-sister thing like helping her younger sister get ready for a date was a precious gift to Jessie, who didn't get a lot of opportunities to do things like that. She'd learned early and quickly how to be an extraordinary big sister, an encourager, a caretaker, and a sister with responsibility. The day of the prom, however, was uncharacteristically silly and fun, and while the experience might have been normal for most people, it wasn't for us. The day of the prom was rare, and we embraced it.

Once fully dressed, she looked so pretty, so grown up, so happy. Before everyone arrived, we Skyped with Jason, who was away at college (she wanted to show him what Jess had done to her hair and face and how she looked in her pretty dress). Then we took some family pictures with her alone; I look at them now and see that prom day was a day we all glowed with pride and satisfaction.

The other families arrived with their kids, and after the always awkward exchange of boutonnieres and corsages, we took pictures in front of the fireplace just as we'd planned. We watched as the kids, not quite sure how close they should stand to their dates, or what they were supposed to do with their arms and hands, arranged themselves. Their smiles and grins were infectious. They instinctively knew how to do this pre-prom thing, and they did it right; not one of them was pretentious, snobby, bored or embarrassed by their parents. They were genuinely thrilled with the attention and the excitement of the night.

The limo arrived, and we walked out to meet it. Curt and a few of the dads had a long talk with the driver while the rest of us helped the kids scramble into the wide open backdoors. The limo's interior, with its purple rope lighting and seats arranged to face each other, was fully equipped with sodas, snacks, music, and televisions, which took their breath away. *"Awesome!" "Incredible!" "Best night ever!"* were the words we heard as they pulled away, leaving us standing there in the street, smiles stuck to our faces, hoping that indeed, the night would continue the way it had begun.

She arrived home around eleven, tired and disheveled; fancy shoes in the bag, flip-flops on her feet. She loved it, she said. She had so much fun. And then said she needed to go to bed, she said that she'd *"hit the wall,"* which was what she always said when she was tired.

Tucking her into bed, I smoothed her hair back from her face with my hand one more time to steal a peek at the grin I knew would be there on her lips. It's the grin that we'd taken note of when she was less than a year old. It's the grin that subconsciously appeared on her face whenever she got into bed at night. She'd had a big day, and a big night, and she was happy to be home. I leaned down to her soft sweet cheek, still covered in a thin coat of pretty pink blush, and kissed her goodnight.

22

Two Years After

EARLY IN THE morning Ivy, the two year old grandbaby who is just learning to put words together to tell us what's on her mind, points to the small gold bracelet that I've placed on her arm again today, waiting for the day it actually fits her, and for the day that she'll actually keep it on. As she points to it, she tells me," Auntie's bracelet," because that's what I tell her each time we try it on. Later that day, she points to a red crayon and tells me, "Auntie's favorite."

Just before lunch, Jack, Ivy's five-year-old brother, tells me, "Nanny, I want to play with a toy at your house that I've never played with before." He knows that will get me digging through the box of toys and favorite things I've saved for these grandkids when they were just imagined. I pull out an old favorite puzzle box, with tattered edges that, like the Velveteen Rabbit, shows just how much it's been loved. From the front of the box Arthur the Aardvark, his sister D.W. and his beloved dog Pal smile up at me, frozen in time. They'll never age, they're still there, ready to play, just as we left them years ago. I sit with the five-year-old, telling him how much his Auntie used to love Arthur, then begin to teach him how to work the puzzle, beginning with the red border and corner pieces first, then moving in towards the middle. And then I remember how I sat, not that long ago working this same puzzle, giving the same instructions to his 21-year-old aunt. I can say with certainty that we've gotten our money's worth out of that puzzle we purchased when she was just ten years old. She never grew tired of it. I know that Jack will, which is good and right, but somehow hurts a little, especially because he'll probably tire of it before the year is out.

I talk a lot about her with the grandkids. I'm careful not to overdo it; I don't want them to think I'm the creepy grandma who never stops talking about her dead daughter. I just slip in facts and stories as they come up because I want them to grow up loving and remembering the Auntie that they never really knew.

I stay at the table and watch Curt stand by the restaurant window holding both Jack and Ivy in his strong arms. Ivy's in the crook of his left arm and Jack's in his right. They are watching the snow fall outside while we wait for our food to arrive. It's February, and we've just come from the crowded rec center where we took the kids to swim indoors this cold winter's day. The rec center was fun and hectic and loud; it seems like everyone thought it the perfect day for a swim. Kids everywhere, half of them screaming, but for us, things went well— no tears, no whining, and nobody was scared. There were two of us and two of them, we divided and conquered. I took the girl, he took the boy; we changed in the locker rooms and met in the pool. We played with the kids in the water for about an hour or so, taking turns staying with Ivy in the baby pool area, who loved splashing in the little waterfalls, or catching Jack as he flew down the slides at the deeper end of the pool. We split up again when it was time to leave, each taking a kid back into the locker room, to get them dressed, then we met up again in the lobby, feeling pretty proud of ourselves, and our grandparenting skills. The kids had a great time, and so did we.

Sitting alone now at the restaurant, watching them watch the snow fall, I think about how much our girl would have loved this day, and how much different the day would have been had she been with us. The day would have still been sweet but would have taken so much more effort, both physical and emotional. The day would have been harder because she'd have wanted to help and would have needed so much help herself. She'd have wanted to help the kids with everything from getting into the car to getting into the pool, and we'd have given her that because we would have wanted to allow her to be the Auntie. And then we would have helped her, and then we would have helped them. The day would have been harder because she'd have wanted to play with the kids in the pool, but would have been out of place, not swift enough or agile enough to dodge a splashing toddler, and not strong enough to tread water in the deep end of the pool while we waited for Jack to come down the slide. We would have helped the little kids, and then would have helped her. We would have watched the little kids show us their pool tricks, and then we'd have watched hers. She would have wanted to help me with Ivy in the locker room, and I'd have let her do what she was able, like pull the clothes from the bag, or dry Ivy's hair with a towel, because that would have made her feel useful and happy. Then I'd help Ivy get dressed, and then I'd help her. I'd place Ivy on her Auntie's lap in the shiny red wheelchair, which would have brought smiles to both of their faces and then I'd wheel them out to the lobby where we'd meet Curt and Jack. She would have been so proud of her little niece and nephew and the fact that they looked to her for help. We all would have had fun, and Curt and I would have been exhausted.

Lost in my thoughts of what might have been, my gaze wanders back to the window where Curt stands with the kids. This time when I look though, I see that there's four of them near the window, not just three. Clear as day, I see our tall girl standing as close to her stepdad as she can possibly get; one of her big hands resting on the back of his neck, the other placed gently on her nephew's shoulder.

She's with me a lot, this girl of mine who is not really here anymore, and that's good with me. I don't dwell on her or drag her around with me. She quietly tiptoes into my heart, my mind, and my soul sometimes, and I welcome her. It's not painful having her around or remembering her, its reassuring and comforting and right. I want to remember everything, and I'm okay imagining what might have been, which brings me back to today, and my seat at the table, where I'll stay for a bit, while I watch the four of them watch the snow fall outside as they stand by the window.

23 | Three Years After

TODAY IS MAY 8. I wish it wasn't. Today is the third anniversary of her death. I wish it wasn't. I wish I could skip May 8th but I can't. I wish May went from May 7 to May 9, but it doesn't.

I begin, just after Easter each year, looking toward May 8th with dread. May 8th is a day of expectation. People expect I'll be sad on May 8th. I suspect the same.

It's Easter when images start rolling on continuous repeat through my mind. I begin by remembering the last Easter she was with us; the lunch we had with extended family, the dress she wore that used to fit snugly, but that year, hung from her thin little frame. I remember the happy tears we cried when Jessie announced that she and her husband Brian were going to have another baby. I remember how there were two wheelchairs present at lunch that day—one for Brian's 90-year-old grandmother and one for our 22-year-old daughter.

A week before the anniversary of her death arrives, I wake up remembering what each day leading to her last looked like, and what each day leading to her last felt like.

Thursday was the day we moved her into the assisted living house. We'd come to the agonizing realization that caring for her at home had become too difficult; we were exhausted; we needed help. Thursday could have been a sad day, but it wasn't. She was eager the day we'd built up for weeks had finally arrived. She was delighted that her room at the assisted living house was the largest room in the whole house, and she was excited to see all of her belongings loaded into the back of the moving truck. When I think about that Thursday, I remember the adorable "look-at-me" grin she couldn't wipe off her face as she rode shotgun in the big moving truck towards her new home.

Friday was the morning we spent making her room the cutest room the assisted living facility had ever seen. - I remember how she sat contentedly in the comfy baby-blue chenille armchair we brought from home because it was her favorite, and I remember how happy it made her when she saw the big gold letters hung over her bed spelling out her name.

Saturday was the day we took her on a plane to see Curt's family. The trip had been planned for a while - a trip to celebrate Curt's dad's birthday. Spending time in the small Minnesota town where Curt grew up was something she adored. Curt's family doted on her in the best of ways by simply including her in all they did. They lived their lives and took her along for the ride, which, when she was healthy and able to spend a week with them each summer on her own, meant doing things like picking corn, petting horses, watching softball games, playing cards and eating ice cream. She was comfortable there and was loved there.

The decision to take her on the trip was one that we wrestled with. Her frail little body was by then deteriorating rapidly. It seemed almost overnight that she couldn't walk even a single step, or hold anything more substantial than her toothbrush in her hand. We knew the most she'd be able to do once we arrived in Minnesota was hang out in the house with the family (which by the way, was fine by her and fine by the family too).

Emotionally she was still the same happy girl; she wanted to go, and we didn't want to disappoint. We discussed at length what we'd do if medical attention became necessary while we were in Minnesota. We came to the hard and honest conclusion that we'd do what we'd decided to do if we were home and medical attention became necessary; we'd keep her comfortable, but nothing more. By that time we'd signed a Do Not Resuscitate.

We decided to take her on the trip. We decided to go to Minnesota.

When I think about Saturday, I relive every detail of that trip. How labor intense it was getting her through the airport and into her seat on the plane, how excited she was when she "beeped" going through security. And how when she was searched (like a potential terrorist - all 110 pounds of her) she sat smiling in her bright red wheelchair, cuddling her favorite little-stuffed dog who looked a lot like our real dog, John Wayne.

I especially remember how happy she was sitting at the kitchen table playing UNO with Curt's mom, and how thrilled she was with the wooden card rack that Grama had bought for her, anticipating that she wouldn't have the strength to hold the cards on her own. I remember she didn't bat an eye (to the fact that we were all) - all except her, going out to dinner to celebrate Grampa's birthday. I remember her being delighted with the fact that family friends were coming over with their six-year-old and three-year-old just to hang out with her until we got home.

When I think about Saturday, I think about love.

Sunday was the day our hearts were hurting because she was becoming weaker and more frail, and there was nothing we could do about it. Sunday was the morning I woke up to text messages that I hadn't seen through the night.

"Mom, i need you." 3:43 AM

"MoM, I need to go potty." 4:00 AM

"No joke mom, I need you." 4:12 AM

"Sorry to brother you mom, I need to go potty." 4:30

For years I slept with the phone right by my bed. For years I got up every time she texted me or called my name. For years I never missed or ignored a text. That Sunday morning in Minnesota, the phone on the night table buzzed repeatedly, and I slept through it. By the time I raced up the stairs at six in the morning, Curt's mom had already discreetly and quietly changed the linens on the bed and helped our girl into clean pajamas.

When I think about Sunday morning, I think about not hearing the phone.

Sunday afternoon was a blur. My dad picked us up from the airport, and I remember noting the distraught look his face held when he saw us, as well as his unsuccessful attempts to hide it from me when he knew I'd noticed. I remember wondering, but not asking, who he was most distraught for. His daughter or his granddaughter?

I remember stopping to get her some food on the way home. I remember sitting next to her in the back seat of the car watching her happily gobble down a piece of greasy pepperoni pizza.

When I think I about Sunday I think about utter exhaustion.

Monday was the day we went to the Rockies game. Upon urgings from the staff at the assisted living house, we agreed to take a break for the day and scrounged up tickets to an after-noon baseball game. Curt went over to the house to check on her before we left. I remember his call telling me that she was fully dressed and in a deep, sound sleep in her big blue chair; it was ten in the morning. I remember him telling me that our girl, who was always so alert, so aware, and so excited to see people, especially him, couldn't be roused. The house staff re-ported that she'd been up that morning and happy as ever. They said they'd keep a close eye on her. We attributed her fatigue to the weekend travel. We all agreed she needed to sleep.

We were told she woke up just before noon, ate lunch and went out with some of the old folks from the house to visit a class of high school seniors. I have pictures of her laughing and handing out gifts to the soon to be graduates with her new 85-year-old friends.

When I think about Monday, I think of her remarkable ability to rally.

Tuesday was the day she had lots of visitors. Laurie was the first to stop by with a vase full of perfectly arranged red flow-ers and a fun piece of art to hang on the wall that included all my girls' favorites, even toy fire trucks. Jessie came next with markers and paper and set to work at helping her sister make a sign with her name on it for the front door of her room. Pop (my dad) brought pie. Jason brought music and laid his head on the pillow next to hers while they listened to it together. Curt brought John Wayne, who claimed his rightful place on the bed with her. Debbie brought Gary, and that alone brought joy to the room. Michelle and Mark brought food from her favorite place Sonic, (or *"Soinc"* as we all called it because of the way she consistently misspelled it). Tammie brought books. Geoff, our friend the doctor, brought a catheter. Kay brought ice cream.

When I think about Tuesday, I think of being blessed.

Wednesday was the day I got the call early in the morning to let me know she was okay but had fallen getting out of bed. I remember rushing to the assisted living house where I found her dressed and ready for the day, excited to show me how pretty her hair looked. After one of the men who worked at the house had picked her up off the floor, an aide had cleaned her up and taken the time to pull her hair back into a beautiful braid, and that's what she was focused on. She wasn't focused on the fact that her legs could no longer support her or that she'd fallen, but instead on the fact that a nice girl had braided her hair and made her feel special.

She wanted chicken nuggets for lunch Wednesday afternoon. I helped her eat them from her big blue chair. Later that day, still sitting in the chair, she slipped into another deep sleep. I called her name. I gently shook her. I rubbed her arms. I put a cool cloth to her head. Nothing I did would rouse her. I called Curt and asked him to come. I almost called 911, but called our friend Debbie (an ICU nurse) instead, who talked me through the very real possibility that this could be the end.

She reminded me that we'd decided there'd be no heroics and no drama. She reminded me that we'd decided upon comfort instead of prolonging the inevitable, and then she asked me if my girl appeared to be in pain. My answer was that she looked peaceful, so Debbie's advice was to sit with my child and love her, and that's what I did. I sat in the big blue chair whispering words of encouragement and sweet memories of how much she was loved, along with the words hospice had advised us to give when the time came, words that assured her that it was okay for her to go.

Wednesday was the day I didn't think she'd wake up, but then she did.

She rallied again. She woke up while Curt was sitting across from us on the edge of the bed, and the hospice nurse we'd just hired stood in the corner talking to Debbie. She woke up without fanfare or fuss. She simply woke up, looked around the room, and then asked us if we'd take her outside so she could show everyone her world famous, super loud, super ridiculous birdcall.

When I think about Wednesday, I think about how naive I was that death was so near.

Thursday was the day I received the call from the house telling me to come immediately. It was seven thirty AM. I was with my sweet friend Amy in a coffee shop and oddly enough remember insisting upon driving to the house because I knew the way.

The house staff house told me she'd woken up that morning, happy and ready to start the day, despite the pummeling thunderstorm the night before that had forced her to wear the noise canceling earphones Gary had given her for just that occasion. Thunder scared her, but she was prepared. She'd texted a picture of herself to a few of us Wednesday night to show us that she was doing okay and following the "rules" we had set up for her. In the picture, she's lying in bed with the clunky army green earphones covering her ears while the CPAP breathing machine mask (she wore because of serious sleep apnea) covered her nose and mouth. Looking closely at the picture, underneath it all, you see a smile on her face.

She was dressed, that morning, by staff at the house and they'd braided her hair again in the style they knew she was so proud of. They brought her out to breakfast to sit at the table with all the old people, her new housemates. From there we aren't sure of the details, but what we do know is this: the kind man, with whom she'd visited the high school kids a few days earlier, and who had taken a liking to her was sitting next to her. When she started to slip out of her chair, he yelled out, *"I think we are losing her."*

From there we surmise that she choked on the pancakes they served that morning for breakfast. Her body too weak to swallow, her arms too weak to pound the table to indicate that something was wrong. In the past, as she became weaker, we'd saved her several times from choking. I'd always been the one to notice that she needed help, and Curt had always been the one to carry out what she referred to as the *"Hindlick Remover."*

When I think about Thursday morning, I think about her sitting at the table.

When I think about Thursday morning, I think about not being there.

When I think about Thursday morning, I think about the staff at the assisted living house following the protocol we'd set up:

no paramedics, no doctors, no heroics.

By the time we got there and opened the door to her room, she had passed. I remember that she was tucked into bed with the little-stuffed dog by her side. I remember the big gold letters spelling out her name hanging over her bed. I remember the intense feeling of needing to be close to her.

When I think about Thursday, I remember pulling back the covers and climbing into bed right next to her. I think about how my head felt laying on her still shoulder and how it felt to drape my arm and leg across her body.

When I think about Thursday, I think of lying with her, one last time, under her favorite red quilt.

Today is May 8th, three years later and I'm aware, more than ever, how the space between us has grown. She feels farther away from me this May 8th than she did the last. I'm not as certain of the sound of her voice, the touch of her hand, or what the everydayness of her felt like. I strive to remember.

Today is May 8th, I wish it wasn't, but it is.

24

Eighteen to Twenty-Two Years Old

I CAN EASILY pinpoint the beginning of the end. It was the summer just after her high school graduation. She was stepping into a new phase of life, which meant we were stepping into a new phase of life as well. We were prepared for change but were caught completely off guard with what came next.

Curt and I were planning to take an unprecedented three-week vacation - just the two of us. We'd rented a house on a lake and were giddy to get away for such a long stretch of time. We were comfortable leaving knowing our business and our kids would be just fine without us.

We made the perfect arrangements for our girl. The first week she'd be in the mountains at a summer camp she loved and had been to every summer since the sixth grade. The second week she'd spend with her dad, and the following week with Kara, her sweet childhood friend who through the years spent time with her after school, and would stay with her at our house while we were gone. Our girl was looking forward to it all.

We took off for the lake house and three days into the trip vowed to make it an annual event.

We talked to her most every day on the phone, and with each phone call, we determined she was having as much fun without us as we were having without her.

At camp, she hiked, rafted, rode horses and roasted marshmallows. She told us how great it was to accompany her dad to his office because the people there really needed her to help them with their work. But, she told us hanging out with Kara was the best.

We lived in a condominium that summer (while we waited on renovations to be completed on our new house), which meant there was a pool just a few feet from our front door. Kara and our girl spent their afternoons poolside and spent the rest of their time together cooking, shopping, crafting and watching movies. Kara said our girl was cheerful and funny and taking very seriously Curt's instructions that she be the "man of the house" while he was gone. She hadn't missed a day of taking out the trash, feeding the dog, or emptying the dishwasher.

Kara also told us that there hadn't been a day without complaint of a headache.

Two days after returning home, I sat with my girl in the neurosurgeon's office at Children's Hospital where she was on the "maintenance plan." We hadn't seen this doctor for five years as she had very few hitches with the shunt that ferried excess fluid away from her brain.

She was one of the lucky ones we were told. A shunt

malfunction required surgery, and she'd only experienced one malfunction in eighteen years. She was seven years old and had been complaining of severe headaches. Her doctors determined the shunt wasn't doing its job. So for the second time in her young life, doctors dove deep into her brain with their tools and instruments, this time to make repairs. They replaced parts and extended tubing, the surgery lasted only an hour. She went home from the hospital the next day, good as new. Her shunt had worked perfectly for the last eleven years.

Headaches were things we took note of. Headaches, we knew, could be an indication something was wrong.

And this time, something was. There was a pocket of fluid in an unexpected spot — a spot at the base of her skull near the top of her cervical spine. Surgeons were hopeful, but not certain, that repairing the shunt would alleviate the situation. They wouldn't know until they went in, and they thought it best to get in right away.

Without much time to think or plan, we accepted the facts we were given and jumped into action. We prepared her by explaining that doctors were going to make her headaches go away. We told her they'd have to shave away a bit of her hair, but that it would grow back. We told her she'd have to spend a couple of nights in the hospital, but that we'd stay with her, and then we'd all go home. We told her that when her transition program (classes she was eager to attend now that high school was over) started up in two weeks, she'd be good to go. We packed up her bag with her favorite red flannel pajamas, her beloved stuffed dog, her phone and her toothbrush. We threw in a few things for ourselves and told her everything was going to be okay.

She believed us, we believed us, and because it was the better of two evils, we prayed the shunt was malfunctioning.

But it wasn't. The shunt was working. There would be no easy fix.

The pocket of fluid was an entirely new problem, something rare, not often seen. A team of doctors would need to go back inside our sweet girl's head the very next day to somehow "decompress" (a word they kept throwing at us like we knew what it meant) the fluid.

The hospital was a teaching hospital and doctors, fellows, interns, and students came out of nowhere to get in on this exciting new case. The process was moving rapidly and was terrifying. Somehow, though, we felt okay about what needed to be done. We trusted the neurosurgeon, we trusted the hospital, and mostly, we trusted the fact that her pain would continue as long as the fluid remained. We trusted the fact there could be serious complications by allowing the fluid to set up shop. We knew we had to let the surgeons have a go at her again.

We told her the doctors had more work to do before they were able to make her headaches go away. We told her they'd be able to finish their job the following day. She didn't sleep in her red flannel pajamas that night. Instead, she slept in the hospital gown she'd worn out of the recovery room. There was no dinner for her that night either; her belly needed to be empty for surgery the next morning. It was a rough night for all of us.

We told her she was going to be okay. She believed us. We believed us.

The following day surgery lasted eight agonizing hours, at least five hours longer than expected. Various doctors and nurses came to talk with us throughout the day. They told us there was an astonishing amount of scar tissue they'd had to move aside or work around, and that the scar tissue was making the job of decompression extremely tedious. Besides this decompression thing, we learned there were little parts of her brain that needed to be shored up and held into place. We learned these little pieces of brain were called tonsils and they were trying to slip into tight areas that weren't meant for brain. They were slipping, apparently, into her spinal cord, thus causing the build-up of fluid.

Twenty-four hours earlier, we'd never heard the word tonsil associated with the brain, and now we were trying to ask intelligent questions and formulate reasonable responses when talking to doctors about what they'd done inside our sweet girl's head.

We sat by her side in recovery. She was wiped out from surgery, her face puffy, and her head bandaged. The word from the docs was that they were pleased with the outcome of the surgery. She would recover. They told us she would be well.

They told us that her headaches would go away … and we believed them.

We spent four nights with her in the hospital room. We tried to get a few hours of sleep either on the recliner that reclined with a mind of its own or on the cot built for parents much shorter than us.

The fifth day we were allowed to take her home to the little condo we were renting. It wasn't our home, but it was home nonetheless. We were glad to be out of the hospital. We told her she'd feel better soon.

She believed us ... and we believed us.

The transition program started without her. She was able to begin attending a few days a week sometime late September, almost two months after her surgery. She didn't have much strength or stamina. What little balance and physical prowess she'd had before surgery had disappeared. She'd lost over twenty pounds. Physically, she'd never again be the girl she had been prior to surgery. Everything about her looked different — the shape of her face, the thinness of her frame, the haircut we'd given her to help hide the bald patch (this time the neurosurgeon did a number on her hair), the way she moved.

Inside though, where it mattered, she was the same. She was still happy. She was still so nice. She was positive. She was eager and trusting and innocent, and she still looked forward to whatever would come next. She was still funny, and loving, and she cared about other people infinitely more than she cared about herself. She was still all of that.

And she still had headaches.

The beginning of the end lasted a year and a half and included:

* six more surgeries (three more decompressions, two more shunt revisions, and finally a spinal fusion)
* a new team of doctors and surgeons
* countless MRIs and CT scans
* fifteen emergency room visits
* countless doctor appointments

* countless therapy sessions, (physical therapy, occupational therapy, Pilates)
* a range of massage sessions (with various practitioners who believed their method of massage was sure to bring relief)
* acupuncture treatments
* dry needling treatments
* sustained hospital stays

We told her throughout the beginning of the end that she'd be okay. She believed us ... we mostly believed us.

The middle of the end involved more of the same and lasted a little over a year. The middle of the end was marked with some pretty great highs and some pretty significant lows. Surgeons dove back into her head and spine ten times more that year. She'd rally for weeks at a time, then her physical weakness would increase. The middle of the end was like a whac-a-mole game — we'd get rid of one problem without a moment to rest before the next problem reared its ugly head.

We told her she'd be okay ... she believed us.

The end of the end came and hung around for about a year. The end of the end is when we decided there would be no more surgeries, no more hospital stays, no more doctor appointments, and no more ER visits. What little therapy she received, she received in our home, in her room, by a trusted physical therapist friend, and served only to reduce her pain. Our efforts at the end of the end were aimed at comfort, not rehabilitation.

We were more realistic at the end of the end. We knew that short of a miracle, as long as she lived, her pain would live with her. At the end of the end, when she'd tell us her head hurt, we did everything we could to reduce the pain, if only for the moment. We stopped searching for a cure. We stopped trying to find answers. It was freeing and in a deja vu sort-of-way brought back memories of how I felt when she was a baby and decided to stop the search for a diagnosis. Back then, we decided to accept instead of analyze. At the end of the end, we decided to sooth instead of fix.

We installed a hot tub and lifted her weak little body in and out of it, allowing the water, the heat, and the simplicity of staying home to give her temporary relief. We medicated (in fact, probably overmedicated) her with whatever legal or illegal substance we could get our hands on. We were there with bags of Doritos and chocolate when she told us the edible marijuana we'd given her had given her the munchies. We loved on her and held onto her and told her how sorry we were that she hurt.

She never questioned us once when we told her she'd be okay.

She believed us at the beginning of the end, the middle of the end, and at the end of the end. That girl knew how to believe, that girl knew how to trust.

The words chiseled beneath her name on her stone in the cemetery so true:

"With quiet strength and trust so complete, she lived with love."

We tell ourselves now that she is okay ... and we believe us.

25

I thought of her last night when...

I WAS JOLTED awake by a book I've been reading about a family during The Holocaust. The book describes in great detail the steadfast way the family's love for each other helped them survive. Before closing my eyes to sleep, I'd read an anguished account of a young mother's desperate attempt to save her daughter.

The jolt that woke me in the middle of the night caused me to feel strange and kind of sick. But not throw-up sick; this was the kind of sick that had my heart racing and my palms sweating. This was the kind of sick that included a bit of nausea, but this sick was more in my head than in my body.

I've known this sick before and been awakened by it before too; in the days my sweet girl still slept in her bedroom down the hall and around the corner from ours.

The sick that jolted me awake last night was a trigger that immediately brought me back to nights I'd fallen into bed exhausted after holding it together all day (pretending I knew what I was doing) while I played doctor, therapist, nurse, teacher, mother, and overall caretaker. The tasks I performed those days were out of my league, but I did them because she needed me to and because I was the mom and that's what moms do.

Getting into bed each night I looked forward to sleep. I'd usually get a few good hours in and then I'd wake, always at 2 a.m. with the perfectly horrible feeling I can only describe as despair.

Despair came only at night, but I knew, if I let it, despair would consume me. I refused to let that happen by doing the only thing I knew to do in the dark of the night; I prayed.

When despair woke me and tried to pull me into the "what-ifs" (what if she falls getting out of bed, what if the pain in her arms and shoulders worsens, what if she loses the use of them completely, what if her fever runs high), I'd remind myself that my worrying made no difference, and I'd recite a psalm of trust I'd been memorizing for these late night encounters. When I awoke with the "whys" of despair (why is this happening to her, why is this happening to me, why can't the doctors help her, why won't God help her) I'd push myself to talk with God and tell him I trusted him, despite what he was allowing to happen to my girl. There in the dark, in the middle of the night, I remember asking God for just an hour of sleep at a time.

Most nights my prayers and chats with God calmed me. Most nights he'd give me that hour-at-a-time sleep I asked for, and I'd thank him for it the next time I woke up. I consciously chose to trust, preferring (I suppose) strength and faith over weakness, defeat, and a permanent chip on my shoulder. Still, I'd wake with despair, but recognize it for what it was, "the complete loss or absence of hope," and choose to run from it for fear that it would envelop me.

Three years ago when she left me, despair left me too, and that sick in the middle of the night feeling hasn't woken me since. Until last night when I read the story of the young Holocaust mother and was reminded again of the perfectly horrible feeling (I'm certain now I'll never forget) of a mother's broken heart.

26

Nineteen Years Old

SHE HAD A boyfriend named Ryan. She met Ryan after we were introduced to his parents by a mutual friend who thought, correctly, that we had a lot in common. Ryan's parents became close friends of ours, and Ryan and our girl became a "thing" pretty quickly after that.

Ryan was older than she was and a little more worldly. She'd hold his hand, and maybe give him a kiss on the cheek now and then, and all of that was more than okay with Ryan, who talked a big talk with the guys about having a girlfriend, but was always a gentleman with her.

They were pretty cute together. Each of them had unsteady gaits and tilted their heads to the side in opposite directions, so when they walked next to each other, it looked almost like each of them was holding the other up. They both had long fingers and hands - the difference was Ryan's were thin and almost delicate where hers were thick and strong even when the rest of her body grew weak.

We lived on opposite ends of town, which made getting

together complicated, so they didn't spend a lot of time together. When they did, they were giddy. Ryan doted on her, which as her mom, was sweet to see. He told her she was beautiful, he held the door for her, he grinned when he looked at her, he put his arm around her. Not knowing exactly how to take all the attention, she reciprocated by giggling, holding his hand, and telling him he was "crazy." They talked on the phone a lot. He was the recipient of oodles of her emails and slideshow presentations.

The two of them went to a dance. The dance was put on by a community organization and was a "prom" for people with disabilities. When Ryan asked our girl to go, she was healthy, but the dance occurred a few months after her first surgery. The day of the event we were trying to determine if she had the stamina to attend. She quickly squashed any idea of her staying home by delivering her often used rationale, "I have to go, Ryan is counting on me."

An hour before the dance began, we met Ryan and his parents at a park near the community center where the dance would take place. We took pictures of the kids and of our families near an old train caboose in the park. Jessie and Brian stopped by and joined in the festivities too. Our girl was impressed by the way Ryan was dressed, in suit pants, a vest, white shirt and red tie. He told her she was the prettiest girl he'd ever seen. We dropped the kids off at the dance and went out to dinner, with our cell phones in hand, ready for the call at any minute telling us to come back and get our girl, because "she'd hit the wall," the phrase she would use when her body was just too weak and tired to go on.

The call didn't come.

When the dance was over, and we went back to collect them, we found them standing together each holding the other up (in their own inimitable way) with crowns on their heads.

They had been named "King" and "Queen" of the prom.

She proudly wore her crown for weeks.

Ryan, like our girl, knew his way around a hospital and was as familiar with being a patient in one as she. Neither made a big deal about being hospitalized, nor about visiting the other while they were there. We spent a lot of time with Ryan's family in our girl's hospital room. They always brought dinner to feed us, cards to entertain us, and whiskey to numb us. We laughed a lot those nights, as we sat with our friends in what would be for most families, a frightening and abnormal place where IV machines beeped, and blood pressure monitors pumped, and computer screens kept track of heartbeats. For the six of us, this was normal, those nights were actually fun, and it meant the world to our girl that her boyfriend had come to visit.

About six months before she died, Ryan was in the hospital; it was her turn to be the visitor. She brought him a chocolate milkshake and handed it to him with a pleased grin. She sat by his bed, and they talked about how being in the hospital *"is no fun."* They commiserated on how it hard it was to sleep and how the food was *"just not that good."* She sat by his bed and held his hand and told him that she hoped he'd be out soon. She sat by his bed and showed him that she was wearing the rhinestone necklace that a few months ago he'd been so very proud to give to her. Ryan laid back in his hospital bed, placed his head on his pillow, and smiled back at her with that very same pleased grin.

Ryan's parents and Curt and I would have placed bets on Ryan being the first to go, but that wasn't the case. Ryan has suffered from seizures, many of them huge, every day of his life since the day he was born. Today Ryan is 33 years old.

27 | Three Years After

MY DAD AND I planted flowers Saturday morning at the graves of my mom and my daughter. We tried our best to act like it was the most normal thing in the world for a father and his daughter to be doing on a Saturday morning, the day before Mother's Day.

Mother's Day for our family isn't what it used to be. My mother died on Mother's Day twenty-one years ago, which pretty much put the kibosh on Mother's Day being a real fun day for us. She died way too young, at fifty-five, a year younger than I am now.

Eighteen Mother's Days later, Jessie and Jason gave me a necklace with three antique keys hanging from it, one key for each of my children's hearts. We buried their sister the very next day.

Whereas some people spruce up their houses for the company that may drop by on Mother's Day, my dad and I spruce up the graves. We know the cemetery will be visited by others in our family on Mother's Day, and we want the place to look nice. (Truth is, we'd make the place look nice even if it was just for the two of us.) But there's something about seeing flowers blooming there on Mother's Day that makes us feel better—even though we were the ones who planted them, just the day before.

The garden store on Saturday was swarming with people who clearly all believe the TV weather personalities who proclaim that Mother's Day weekend is THE WEEKEND to plant flowers in Colorado. Somewhere in the maze of folks scrambling to find the perfect daisies for their yard, I found my dad, whose gift for being positive is legendary. He was pushing a faded flat-bed cart looking somewhat faded and lost himself. His posture at eighty-two is a little stooped, and to me, on that day, his countenance seemed stooped as well.

I'd visited the cemetery already early that morning to determine which of the plants had made it through winter and which needed to be replaced. I knew, kind of, just what we'd need to purchase, and that was good; I didn't want to prolong our time at the greenhouse any longer than necessary. My dad was overwhelmed, which had me wondering if this year - our Mother's Day tradition - was too much for him.

My dad has always been a happy man; he's one of those rare people who know how to be satisfied even in the face of great sadness. He is the first to offer a smile, a hug and a joke. Yet his eyes are usually the first to fill with tears of empathy because also he's a tender man. My dad's a big guy, over six feet tall, with a head of thick silver hair that he swears is still black. He's been alone now for twenty-one years. He and my mom were so in love, and he still is. It's harder these days to distinguish between the toll that age is taking on him and the toll that lonesome is taking on him.

Lonesome let go of my dad for a while that day and allowed me to engage him in the hunt for the perfect plants. We zigged and zagged our way through the store and placed things on the cart, only to remove them a few minutes later when we stumbled across something even better. We talked about which flowers we'd get and for whom. We acted like it would really make a difference to my mom and to my daughter which flowers we put where. We acted like the flowers were a gift for them to see and to smell and to enjoy when really this whole charade was about purchasing the flowers for ourselves. We purchased them to make us feel better, we purchased them to make Mother's Day feel better. We said things like, "Oh, look at these, these would make her happy because they are red." And, "How about these purple dahlias, they'd be perfect for Mom, she'd love them." Anyone overhearing us would have thought we were the most thoughtful of all gift givers, and in fact, maybe we were.

We followed each other to the cemetery and parked our cars in the shade alongside the curb. We carried our supplies the hundred feet or so to where my girl (his granddaughter), and his wife (my mom) are buried just a few feet apart. I followed behind him on those trips back and forth to the car, trying not to think about the slowness in his step or the way his whole body seemed to stoop.

We laid out our pretty flowering plants according to plan. The red flowers at the smaller stone, which will always bear only one name, and the purple flowers at the larger stone where there is room, next to my mom's name, for my dad's to be added. We set to work digging (which in a cemetery is always sort of a weird thing to do) the small holes for the new plants.

Digging, we came across some pretty spectacular beetles.

When my dad made me promise and say out loud that when his body was under the ground with my mom's, I'd use a strong pesticide to keep the bugs away, I knew without even glancing that the weary look I'd seen on his face in the garden store had disappeared.

When we were finished, the flowers looked bright and happy and beautiful. The work we did that day was good. Good and weird and comforting and upsetting all at the same time. We acknowledged the mix of emotions but didn't dwell on them. We both knew that what we were doing was for us, and that it was right. Planting flowers, being together, joking, remembering and holding each other up when the other was feeling weak was precisely what we both needed. We stood for a while and surveyed our work arm in arm. We knew that for us, this was the most normal thing in the world for a father and his daughter to be doing the Saturday morning before Mother's Day.

28

I thought of her today when...

I FOLLOWED A mother and her daughter down the cereal aisle in the grocery store. The mother looked close to 70 years old; her daughter, around thirty-seven or thirty-eight. The mother was old-school. Dressed sensibly, not fashionably. She roamed the grocery store in beige rubber-soled shoes and wore a short-sleeve, button-down shirt neatly tucked into the elastic waist of her navy blue slacks. Her grey hair was cut short, her brown purse hung high over her shoulder.

The daughter was a younger version of the mother. She was sensibly dressed, too. Her hair was cut short; her elastic waist pants were tan, her rubber-soled shoes were black. Instead of carrying her brown purse over her shoulder as her mom did, she chose to grasp hers by its short handles and carry it in the palm of her left hand.

The mother was thinner than the daughter. The daughter had that doughy look so many people with disabilities get as they grow older due to a lack of physical activity. The mother looked tired. She looked like shopping this store with her daughter was a drill she'd done so many times before she could do it with her eyes closed.

The daughter scouted the shelves for the perfect cereal.

The mother waited.

The mother helped, she made suggestions.

The mother was kind.

The daughter was proud of herself: she reached the cereal she wanted from the top shelf.

I watched.

I remembered.

I thought about how tired I'd look in another fifteen years.

I smiled at the mother and high-fived the daughter.

29

Twenty-One Years Old

WITH OUR LAST hospital stay three weeks behind us, we felt like we always felt after a hospital stay—that the reset button had been pushed. The surgeons were pleased with their latest construction project, which once again had been funded by insurance, to repair the bones supporting her brain and neck. Doctors told us her spinal fluid highway had been cleared of debris and detours, and that both north and south bound traffic would flow freely. They said they didn't anticipate rush hour jams, even at the dreaded cervical spine interchange.

We were home, and despite a track record that proved otherwise, believed the surgery just completed would be her last. We were sure that when she healed, and we just knew she would, her headaches would be gone. We knew the muscles pulling and pushing and twisting her vertebrae would loosen their grip. We didn't doubt she'd regain the ability to lift her arms, nor did we doubt the fact she'd again be strong enough to walk with confidence. We looked forward to the day again soon when she'd be able to walk into the kitchen, reach up into the cabinet, pull down a glass, fill it with milk and a spoonful of chocolate, stir it up and lift it to her mouth where she'd be able to tilt her head back (no straw needed) and gulp down the chocolatey treat. We could see her set the glass down on the counter with a triumphant thud, and we could imagine the satisfied "ahhh" that would escape from her lips.

We lived with hope.

After each surgery, hospital stay or setback, we delighted in her recovery and found hope in the small. We cheered when she asked us for a "Hot Pocket" sandwich, we marveled when she had the strength to use a fork again; and we loved the fact that she made us laugh.

We always had hope for another good day.

We managed to hang on to that hope almost every day because we believed that God was good and because we had each other. She lived with hope because to her, there just was no other way. She and Curt were the leaders of our little hope parade; they lived with their glasses half full. On occasion, and when necessary, I was able to step forward and take the lead. My march, although usually lockstep, fell at least one pace behind. Our hope fed off of each other, and hope fueled our family.

So it was with hope that we were home again from the hospital and trying to live, or maybe pretending to live, like normal people. It was a Monday afternoon, and I was on the main floor of our house returning business calls, doing laundry, making dinner, and scheduling the week's appointments. Curt was on the upper floor working from his home office. She was in her room watching her favorite TV show, ER. I walked down the four steps to her bedroom and heard the familiar voice of Dr. Green dramatically proclaim "CODE BLUE" and that he was going to use "THE PADDLES."

My sweet girl was propped up in her big, baby blue chenille chair surrounded by cozy pillows, just the way she liked. She'd seen this particular episode of ER at least ten times, so she knew what was going to happen. (I never completely understood her love of that show except for the fact that - because she'd been through so much herself - she felt a particular bond with the actors and the action taking place on the screen.) Her favorite line to medical staff as they described a procedure they needed to administer on her was, *"It's okay...... I'm used to it"*. And she was - because of personal experience and also because she watched medical dramas over and over again on TV.

She was a self-proclaimed expert on all things hospital. On a trip one summer, visiting Curt's parents, his dad had a medical emergency, which instinctively Curt's parents tried to shield from her. Making it clear to them that she was not going to be shielded or pushed aside, she chose to sit by Grandpa's side and share with him her wisdom on what to expect.

She was in her element when she was in the hospital, and watching ER at home was what she liked to do. I was thankful for those shows. Her visits to Chicago General gave me a bit of free time.

"Stand Back, CLEAR," I heard Doc Green shout. I looked to see her enthusiastic reaction and saw something wasn't right. Not on the television, but right there in the big, blue chenille chair. The color had drained from her face, her eyes were droopy, and she was slumped back in an awkward position. I could feel the heat radiate from her body as I reached to touch her skin. I didn't have the strength to pull her forward, and she had no strength at all.

I yelled upstairs to Curt to call for an ambulance.

The DVD continued to play as the paramedics arrived at our house; the patient on the screen wasn't responding. The patient in the big blue chair, however (worse off physically than I'd ever seen her), was so emotionally thrilled by the arrival of the paramedics and the fact they were actually in her bedroom, could not stop smiling. All those firemen there for her, in her house, made her crazy-happy.

Assessing her needs didn't take long. The guys loaded her onto a stretcher and into the back of the ambulance in no time. Curt rode with her ("Only one parent allowed in the ambulance, ma'am"). I took my place in this little parade behind the flashing lights and followed behind in my car. The only sound I heard was the sound of the siren making its way through the evening air.

We knew from past experience that when paramedics flipped the lever to initiate "lights and sirens," it meant business; there was no time to waste. Following the ambulance, I fought to hold back the panic. Inside the ambulance, Curt tells of the shivers that ran up his spine the minute the lever was switched.

To our sweet girl, lights and sirens were adrenaline, and adrenaline, like hope, is a powerful drug. It wasn't long before she was pulling aside the oxygen mask and attempting to adjust the IV needle they'd stuck into her arm so she could sit up and offer suggestions about the fastest route to the hospital and which door she thought would be best to enter. Lights and sirens, to her, were thrilling.

Curt remembers his shivers turning into smiles and how the paramedics smiled too, as this girl, so gravely ill, demonstrated how to live by living every moment. He recalls the ambulance whining and racing through the city streets while the girl on the gurney inside the ambulance slowed things down by sharing tender moments of peace and pure joy.

Standing alone on the curb, waiting for the ambulance doors to open, I thought about how happy she'd be knowing she was arriving via ambulance to her hospital, at the same time Doc Green (who we'd left playing on the DVD player at home), was probably waiting for an ambulance to arrive at his. The back doors of the red and white vehicle opened, Curt jumped out, took one look at me and knew immediately what I needed. He grabbed my hands and shared with me the story he'd just experienced.

Together then, and armed once more with hope, we followed our contented girl (now the leader of our little parade) and the paramedics who pushed her down the corridor we'd walked so many times before to the emergency room where doctors stood ready to treat her. Again, I couldn't help but think about how happy she'd be to know that at home, on the TV in her room, Doc Green was probably waiting in his ER, at just that moment, to begin treating his new patient too.

30

Twenty-Two Years Old

THE PHONE CALLS I made to nursing homes when we suspected the end was near were the most difficult and upsetting phone calls I've ever had to make. I made those phone calls from bed, in my shade-drawn room, underneath a mountain of blankets. I forced myself to make those unfathomable phone calls two mornings in a row, toward the middle of April, when the little purple crocuses planted near the front door of our house began to peek out from under the snow announcing the arrival of Spring.

The calls were difficult because my daughter's condition had worsened and would continue to do so, and by the fact (both hard for me to accept and admit) that caring for her at home was too much. But the calls became even more painful and discouraging when the person on the other end of the line discovered my daughter was just twenty-two years old and had developmental delays. Her young age was an anomaly for these facilities (who cared for the infirm), but her developmental delay was the issue that made the person on the other end of the line squirm.

They would not take her. They could not help us.

I'd stood beside her on uneasy ground like this before, not often thank goodness, but often enough that I immediately recognized the politely coded words that meant, "due to her differences she would not be welcome."

The first time this occurred I was looking for daycare for her, just two days a week for four or five hours a day. She was a curly headed, physically healthy two-year-old. She wasn't walking on her own then, and she communicated mostly through signs and gestures. But her eyes lit up when she smiled, which was most of the time, and she loved looking at books and playing with blocks. Everywhere she went, she carried two tiny stuffed dolls, one of Ernie and one of Bert.

It was clear though that she looked different and acted differently from other two-year-olds and the daycare providers wanted to know why. They wanted to know her diagnosis, her label. When I explained we didn't have one, and that her disabilities had not been identified, I was usually met with sympathetic stares.

When I explained what we did know — that she was healthy and happy and easy, that she ate and drank like a typical two-year-old, and that she understood most everything we said, they wanted to know why she wasn't talking.

When I told them she rarely cried and liked to play with other kids, they wanted to know why she wasn't walking.

When I told them she was receiving therapies to address her delays and that I had no expectations that she "learn" while she was at daycare (that what I was after was just a break a few hours a week). I got the impression I was a terrible mother.

When I told them her hydrocephalus was under control and explained the importance of notifying me if she ever seemed excessively sleepy, lethargic, or had a headache, we were turned away with words like, "We aren't equipped," "Not enough staff," and "Liability."

Discouraged by the reactions I received from public daycare centers, I turned to home providers. I thought they'd be less rigid and more accommodating. I was wrong. And then I remembered a lady I'd heard about who did daycare out of her home less than a mile from us. Her kids were in class with my older kids. (In fact, since she had eleven kids, she probably had a kid in every class.) I inquired about her and checked her references and learned she was well liked.

I called her. I told her everything. She wanted to meet us to determine if we'd be a good fit.

I carried my curly headed girl up the long walk to her big green house. She answered the door wearing a cream-colored cotton blouse and corduroy pants the same color as her house. She had porcelain skin and a rosy smile. She was warm to my girl and business-like with me. We sat on the floor in her playroom surrounded by toys and books all neatly arranged in baskets and bins. We played with the toys she'd set out for us and chatted to get to know each other. After about an hour, she told me she'd call the next day to let me know her decision.

On my way out the door, I noticed a painting of an angel and smiled because the angel was smiling. I was sure this was a sign, and there was no way this mother of eleven, childcare provider extraordinaire, would be daunted by watching my two-year-old with developmental delays.

She called the next day, and her answer was … yes! She'd watch my girl twice a week, four hours a day. She called on a Friday and said we could start the following Monday. I went to sleep that night thinking the world was good.

Saturday afternoon she called and told me she'd had a change of heart.

I could barely make out her words through the sound of my heartbeat pulsing through my ears. I felt sick, sad, hurt and mad. The words she turned us away with were words like, "Not equipped," "Liability," and "Just too much."

I heard those same words again, twenty years later in my shade-drawn room, when the assisted living facilities turned us away for the same reasons.

When I'd explain to providers she had a degenerative issue in her spinal cord that had twisted and bent things so severely her spinal fluid couldn't flow properly, and that she'd had twenty-two surgeries over the last four years, and that now we were just trying to keep her comfortable, they listened sympathetically.

When I explained that she couldn't walk any longer, or lift anything that weighed more than a few ounces, they heard me.

When I told them she had a catheter and that she needed help eating, dressing, sleeping, showering and had several medications that needed to be administered throughout the day, they understood.

Still, they said there was no room at the inn for a child like mine. They helped the elderly; they didn't know what to do with a twenty-two-year-old child.

We were drowning in despair and physical exhaustion trying to keep her comfortable and alive.

On a lead from our family pediatrician, who still helped me out with advice when he could, I called a private home in a neighborhood not far from ours that functioned as an assisted living facility. The woman on the other end of the line heard my anguished voice and truly listened. When I finished my story, she told me she had a heart for kids with special needs. She told me she had a grandson with Down's Syndrome. She told me she was going to help me. She told me her home had never had a young resident before, that she'd never had a person with developmental delays before, but she told me that somehow she would help, and she did.

She and her assistant came to our home to meet us, a few hours later. When she arrived, she put her arms around me and held me and then spent the whole afternoon getting to know us. She was kind and loving to our girl, and she was kind and loving to me. On her way out the door, she hugged me tight and told me it would be an honor to care for our sweet girl. She smiled before she left, and closing the door I smiled too, content I'd received a smile from a true angel.

Two weeks later, we moved our girl into the last place she would ever live.

31

One Year After

SEATED AT A friend's backyard dinner party, the man next to me turns and asks me how many kids I have. Completely unaware how this simple little question messes with me, he waits for my answer.

My brain rushes ahead. How do I answer him honestly without going into all the gritty details? How do I talk about my children and not talk about her? How much do I want to share tonight? This guy is just making small talk: is he ready for something that could go deep? The truth is, I have no idea how to brush over the fact that we used to have three children and that now we have two. Crazy-making I know, but this simple little question has the ability to keep me from wanting to talk to and meet new people.

This question stings.

I'm an approachable person: people tell me they like talking to me because I'm real, I'm honest. My parents encouraged my brother and me to speak from our hearts and minds. We grew up feeling our voices were heard. We were taught to be respectful and to be true. I remember that my parents were impressed and pretty happy when, as a second-grade student, I wrote a candid review of a teacher. Misspellings and all, I talked about the reasons I liked this teacher and the reasons I didn't. My parents' belief was the teacher had asked for an honest evaluation and I gave it. More important to them though was the fact that I signed my name. To this day I never fill out an evaluation or assessment without including my name. I like telling the truth: I value sincerity. It's not my style to hold back, especially to protect myself. I'm wishing now, while the man seated next to me waits on my answer, that it was more in my nature not to wear my heart on my sleeve, not to worry so much about being honest. In fact, I'm learning at 54 years of age that sometimes holding back is a good thing.

Formulating my answer and weighing my options, thoughts bounce and collide in my head like an old game of pinball.

Should I tell him I have three kids?

If I do, he'll ask me how old they are, and then it will begin. The rest of the conversation I'm not sure I want to have.

Should I lie and say two?

That's not really a lie … but saying two feels so wrong. Saying two out loud sounds like I'm saying her life didn't matter, that it was insignificant. Saying two out loud sounds like I'm saying I've forgotten her, or that I've moved on.

I'm never going to forget her, but I'm trying to move on.

When will I discover how to go forward with grace and

ease?

There's this weird thing I find myself doing when I have to tell people the story of our daughter's illness and about our last few years since her death. Once I've shared it all, I hear myself so often sputter something stupid like, "It's okay, it really is," when it most certainly is not.

Sometimes I hear myself saying, "Well, to be honest, we lost our youngest daughter two years ago." (Why do I say lost? Why don't I just use the word died? Do I say it to soften the blow? To soften the blow for whom? This stranger or for me? And why?) After I tell them we lost our daughter, I watch as whoever I'm talking to realizes it's not that I've misplaced my daughter, but that she is dead. I watch as they figure out what to do with the social grenade I've just tossed into their lap, and that's the point where polite dinner party chatter can turn awkward. That is where I usually try to make it all okay by telling a sweet story about who she was, or I say something encouraging about my family and the way we loved her or how we are handling things since her death. I sort of hate consoling this other person, yet I do it time and time again. My rationale goes something like this: I know the story I am about to tell, I'm ready for it, these poor unsuspecting people aren't.

Through trial and error I've discerned that, for now, it's best for me to carry her story quietly inside me, and share it only with whom I chose and when. I'm figuring out that telling just part of her story is okay too; I can give up as much or as little about her as I'm comfortable with. I'm deciding that giving myself permission to hold back, when the time or the place or the person doesn't feel right, is okay ... my act of omission is neither a sin nor dishonoring.

This story I carry is fragile and precious; I keep it protectively wrapped near my heart. I'm careful not to taint it or mistreat it. This story has become mine to tell or not.

In an instant, my answer to the man at the dinner party becomes perfectly clear. "I have three children, two who live very near, and one far away. How about you?"

32

Twenty-Two Years Old

SHE HAD A headache that night. It seems like that last year of her life, she always had a headache. Nothing we found would relieve her pain. Not the twenty-two surgeries she'd undergone over the previous four years. Not the stockpile of prescription drugs we had stashed in the cupboards under our bathroom sink and above our cooktop in the kitchen. Not the weekly massages we took her to. Not the acupuncture treatments she endured. While her physical therapist had The Midas Touch and was able to give her some relief, even that was short lived. Nothing touched her pain for long, not even the edible "pot-candies" that she said made her "*loopy*."

Never one to complain, or put words to her pain, partially because pain was routine for her, and partially because she didn't know how to describe the abstract, when asked what her pain felt like or how bad it was, she'd simply show us. She'd grab a couple of our fingers with both of her big meaty hands, squeeze them together as tightly as she could and screw her face into a big grimace. For added effect, she'd utter a deep-throated *"Grrrrr,"* her way of letting us know the pain was bad.

She'd utter her famous reply, "It's okay,......I'm used to it," when we'd tell her how very sorry we were that she was hurting, and she meant it. She was used to it. And the other thing she was used to, and sure of, was that we'd take care of her. She trusted us with her pain like she trusted us with everything.

So. It fell to us to figure out what to do. It fell to us to know when to try a bath, or a nap, or food, or drink. It fell to us to figure out which narcotic cocktail we should whip up for her. We were the ones to figure out if we should call the doctor and which doctor that should be. At times we had to recognize that we were in over our heads and face the choice of calling an ambulance or taking her to the Emergency Room ourselves. The Emergency Room was a place of last resort for us. We'd learned, from so many previous visits, just how the ER worked. The ER was slow. The ER was crowded. The ER looked to fix what they could immediately, and clearly, she wasn't an immediate fix. We knew that the ER meant a CT scan, or an MRI, which would take hours. We knew the good doctors in the Emergency Room would be stumped by her case. Choosing to make a trip to ER meant that we were desperate and needed two things; 1. a strong dose of something that would knock her out for a while to give her some relief, and 2. a strong dose of reassurance for us that there was no new pressure twisting or pinching her frail little spine or building up inside her innocent little brain.

But for her, the Emergency Room was none of these things. In fact, she kind of loved going to the ER and considered herself an expert on the place. She based her expertise on the personal experiences she'd had in the ER and on the hundreds of experiences she'd witnessed first hand, binge-watching (over and over again) all 15 seasons of her revered TV show. She felt right at home in the ER. The visits usually perked her up so much that we had to warn her countless times that if she didn't act as sick as she really was, we were not going to be happy people. She was always a model patient, compliant and kind.

It was seven o'clock in the evening by the time I determined that the headache she suffered that day was different from the rest. By seven thirty, she'd lost all the color from her face and was becoming unresponsive. By seven forty-five, Curt was wheeling her through the familiar ER doors, with me following behind carrying the oversized canvas bag that we kept stocked for just these occasions with candy, games, water bottles, knitting, an iPad, books, extra clothes, stuffed animals, toothbrushes, phone chargers, and a standby bottle of wine. We'd learned early on that wine came in handy when things got tough, or late, or boring, or scary.

This Emergency Room visit was no different from the rest—she was happy, we were tired. The doctors gave her a strong shot of something to subdue her pain and the MRI, thank goodness, showed nothing new. At 2:30 AM, we were ready to go home. The ER doctor, reluctant to let us leave for fear that we'd be back once the medication wore off, finally agreed to discharge her but wanted to check her vital signs one last time. That's when things went from calm to chaotic.

In a matter of minutes, she was whisked from the exam room to the Intensive Care Unit by a bunch of people wearing yellow gowns, masks, and hats. She was in septic shock, a life-threatening bacterial condition. We had just packed up the oversized canvas hospital bag, we were on our way out the door. We thought we were going home. We thought she was okay. It was difficult to comprehend that we were now wearing the sterile yellow gowns and masks and hats too, and that we were crammed into an elevator holding on to the gurney she was being transported on telling her that everything would be okay.

Our dear friend Debbie was working her shift as an ICU nurse at the hospital that night. She'd been keeping tabs on us in the Emergency Room and knew we were on our way to her unit. Graciously, she took charge of us and of her new patient expertly hooking her up to all sorts of tubes and machines. She managed to make our girl feel safe, and she also managed us, the two grown people frozen by the bedside, feeling completely helpless. She got us some chairs, and she got us some answers. But probably best of all, she was able to get her new patient in the ICU the room with the big window that looked directly onto the hospital's helipad, which sat just a few feet away on the other side of the glass. Our girl hoped for a room facing the helipad every time she was admitted to the hospital but was never given one. Like her affinity for the TV show ER, she had a thing for helicopters too, and the Flight For Life Helicopters, in her mind, were the cream of the crop.

Mornings when we took her to school, we passed by a hospital with a helipad she could spot from the highway. The highlight of the drive began about a mile from the hospital. She'd focus a steady gaze on the hospital campus to look for signs the helicopter was on its pad. Seeing it made her squeal with delight, hold her hands to her chin, and bounce up and down in her seat. Not seeing it made her eager for the afternoon ride home when she could look for it again.

Curt stopped with her a time or two to talk with the Flight for

Life crew and to take her picture in front of the big flying machine. Her dad had even taken her for a chartered ride over the city one day which thrilled her. Helicopters flew over our house quite often, and like Radar O'Reilly from MASH, she'd hear them coming and be able to tell us if we were about to see the blue one, the green one, or the orange one. She sat now in a hospital bed, pale as a ghost, limp as a rag doll, and happy as a clam because just outside her window sat a helipad.

The busyness of getting her hooked up and settled into her room subsided. Antibiotics were already at work pursuing the bacteria that raced through her body. Her heart, blood pressure, temperature, oxygen level, and blood counts were being carefully monitored. We were told that recovery could be slow and that recovery wasn't a sure thing. All we could do was wait.

Somewhere around 5:30 in the morning, after a couple hours of sleep, she heard it … the sound of the bright green helicopter. Working quickly to untangle her from the cords and tubes and bedcovers that surrounded her, we placed her in a wheelchair, and pushed it right up to the glass where she sat mesmerized, eyes and mouth wide open, watching the landing of the chopper. We watched with her, each of us lost in our own thoughts. Her thoughts, I'm sure, were about how great it was to be that close to the action, my thoughts aching for the patient and the family of the person being airlifted to the hospital, and Curt's thoughts on something else entirely. He left the room after a while and returned later with a tall, thin, bald-headed man, who happened to be wearing a navy blue flight suit. Curt had come back to the room with the helicopter pilot.

I watched as the man I adored introduced the pilot to the girl who was fighting for her life. Her eyes lit up when he crouched down beside her and settled in for a face-to-face chat. She was awestruck, a superhero had come to her room for a visit. They talked about the helicopter, they talked about the hospital, they talked about her getting better. He told her he thought she was brave, she told him she thought he was cool.

Exhaustion and the trauma of the day finally overcame us. The pilot left. We gingerly lifted her back into bed and arranged all the cords and tubes and bedcovers around her. We closed the window blinds and turned down the lights; a room down the hall had been set up for us to sleep in. We were afraid to leave her side but knew that sleep was necessary and that the days ahead were going to be hard. We kissed her good-night and headed for the door when she stopped us to say,—- *"today was the best day of my life."*

PostScript- She rallied in the ICU; she wasn't ready to call it quits. A week and a half later we were home, helping her open a brown paper package full of Flight for Life goodies: a water bottle, a sticker, some pens, a t-shirt and a handwritten get well card from her favorite superhero, the pilot.

33

I thought of her today when....

I GOT DRESSED and chose to wear a necklace she made me in ceramics class when she was about 18 years old. She made the two-inch, almost circular beads out of clay. There were five of them, unevenly glazed by her heavy hand in various shades of turquoise. Once fired, she strung them on a long piece of thick twine. Someone must have helped her fasten the twine together in a big fat knot.

I remember when she handed me the little package wrapped in a mess of white tissue paper and announced she had made me a gift.

Gift giving was a specialty of hers. She did it well, taking genuine pleasure in the give. The trouble she had was keeping her gifts a secret, both what they were, and where they were hidden. *"Don't look under my bed or under my pillow or in the bottom drawer of my desk - there's nothing there."* When we opened gifts from her, she'd bounce up and down with excitement while she watched us and inevitably blurt out something like, *"You are really going to like this book!"* ......*(or shirt, or lotion, or box of candy).*

So I wasn't surprised when she asked me to open the little bundle of tissue paper, that she'd told me not to look for under her pillow. I wasn't surprised that inside the tissue paper I found a necklace that she'd already told me I was going to love. The surprise was, that I truly liked the necklace—not just because she'd made it for me, but because I actually liked it. It looked kind of hip and cool, and like something you'd find in a city boutique. The fact that she'd made it was the bonus. How proud we both were when I wore it, and when I received a compliment on it, both of our faces shone with delight.

In those weird moments when you think about what to grab if your house was burning down, I've made a mental note to grab the necklace with the glazed turquoise beads that hang from the piece of worn twine that's held together in the back by a big fat knot.

34

Twenty to Twenty-Two Years Old

HER NIGHTS BEGAN early. By the time she was twenty, a six pm bedtime wasn't out of the question. Life was hard then; her body so very tired.

She communicated her needs from bed to us via text message. Some nights we'd receive more than fifteen different texts to let us know that her arm hurt, or her head hurt, or that she was stuck in an uncomfortable position and wanted to be moved, or that she had to go to the bathroom, or she couldn't find her stuffed animal. Still, we were thankful for the iPhone, it was her lifeline.

She couldn't sleep, so we couldn't sleep. We'd worn the path well, from our bedroom to hers. I began to take a sort of weird delight in my ability to get to her in the middle of the night without turning on a light. Our route could be completed in about 52 paces; down four steps, shortcut through the laundry room, then just a few steps more to the doorway of her bedroom. When we'd get to her, we'd remedy her situation, for the moment at least, and head back to our room through the laundry room, and up the steps where we'd fall into bed until the phone next to our bed buzzed with another request. Nights were long when we considered the time we spent awake, but incredibly short when we counted our hours of sleep.

Every evening her tuck-in to bed began with a series of tasks that needed to be completed before we could shut her door, walk away, and breathe a sigh of relief for the unknown amount of downtime we were about to receive.

The bedtime regimen looked something like this:

First, we'd help her pick out PJs, which usually consisted of pants that were big, baggy, and flannel with dogs or popsicles or snowflakes or flowers printed on them. At night her feet got cold, so she wore socks to bed. She saw no reason for her socks to match. Most nights she'd sport a bright colored tie-dyed sock on one foot and a polka dot or striped sock on the other. On top, she always wore a South Metro fire department t-shirt, of which she had many, due to the number of times we visited the South Metro firemen. She'd been a regular visitor to our neighborhood fire station since she was five years old and never turned down an opportunity to stop in and say hello. She knew every station and station number within a 10-mile radius of our house. We'd see a truck on the street, and she'd shout out the station number and tell us just which truck they were driving, *"that's the ladder truck," "that's the hazmat," "that's the new truck," "look at those wheels!"*

Picking out what to wear for bed was fun for her because she knew that I'd let her wear whatever she wanted to, which is something I didn't do during the day. During the day I thought it important that she look good, important that she fit in. During the day when she was out of the house, I felt that people judged her on so many levels, I wasn't going to let her clothing be a source of that judgment in a negative way. I wanted her clothing to help her stand out positively. I always made sure that she was put together properly before she left the house.

At night though, all bets were off, she got to wear just what she wanted, and she would have loved nothing more than to wear fire station t-shirts 24/7. And this is where it gets tricky for me, and this is where regrets have a tendency to creep in. Why didn't I just let her wear those damn t-shirts when she wanted to……..what harm could it have done……..? And this is where I need to stop myself from thinking about the things I could have, or should have, done differently.

We'd help her into her PJs, her arms and legs at times so weak we'd have to move them for her. I had it down to a science, knowing when to have her lay down and when she was able to sit up and help me. I'd figured out just the right way to put my arm through the sleeve of her t-shirt, grab on to her arm and somehow pull it through. I knew how to sit her on the side of the bed working her pants high enough on to her legs so when I had her lay down, she'd have just enough strength to lift her hips up to get the pants where they needed to be. It's incredible how heavy an arm or leg can be when you're trying to move it without the help of its owner.

A lot of those nights I rubbed her down with lotion. She liked that. Rubbing those flat, thick feet and undefined legs of hers, legs that were about the same width from ankle to knee, with the fruity smelling lotion she preferred, then up to her model-thin hips and ultra flat stomach, finally reaching her long back with its pointy sharp shoulders, I'd realize how thin she'd become.

Growing up she was not thin. She loved to eat, but I limited what she ate. It was important to me that she look good, important to me that she fit in. It was important to me that we didn't add another thing to her list of differences or things to be made fun of. And here again is more regret, ... how bad would it have been if I'd let her eat all she wanted? Again, I cannot think of what I should have or could have done differently.

Once in her pajamas, we'd help her amble to her bathroom where we'd brush her teeth and wash her face. At twenty years old, she was not able to adequately perform these tasks herself. She'd never been a superstar or even proficient at self-care, but she got by with a little help from me each day, and we made accommodations: trips to the dentist every three months for proper cleanings, showers twice a week instead of every day, and lots of ponytails and braids instead of blowdrying and brushing. The last year or so of her life we merely did all of her self-care for her; everything that is, which meant all types of hygienic care.

I added new skills and titles to my resume: bath and shower giver, shaver of legs and *"underpits,"* as she called them, hairdresser, masseuse, dental hygienist, dermatologist, podiatrist, and manicurist. There were times she had catheters, so I learned how to empty and clean and change those when needed. She slept with a BiPap machine (a machine with a mask sort of like an oxygen mask that blew air into her lungs to help with her severe case of sleep apnea). Cleaning that thing out each morning and night was another of the pretty gross jobs I took on, although Curt helped me with that one at least once a week. Through it all every month, she'd received the ultimate injustice - she'd get a period. Why she continued to get them every month or get them at all seemed a cruel twist of fate. Nevertheless, this too was something that we devised a way for me to take care of.

None of this bothered her, none of this made her uncomfortable. She allowed it all, she accepted it all, she was sweet and cute and incredibly compliant. She'd ask for my help with things that would make the average person blush or recoil. We didn't really talk about any of these things being unusual or odd, we just did them because they needed to be done.

I remember feeling like I was living two lives back then; that in addition to my own, I was living hers as well. I'm certain that I took better care of her body those days than I did my own. She didn't worry or think about her stuff; I did. Staying one step ahead was my job. She relied on me because she knew she could, and I was satisfied knowing I was the one we both chose to take care of her in such an intimate way.

As easy going as she was, she had definite ideas on how things needed to be when she actually got into bed. First off, the BiPap mask had to be perfectly fitted to her face, which makes perfect sense. The thing that was hard to understand was just how she kept that mask on the entire night without complaint. She loved the mask and machine from the first night it was brought to her. She liked the technician who brought it to our house and taught her how to use it. We even think she thought the mask was kind of cool. The technician's name was Charles Brown - we called him Charlie even though we're pretty sure he preferred Charles. She liked Charlie Brown, and she liked the attention she received from him. She liked the fact that we had to order new parts for the machine now and then. She liked receiving them either in the mail or in person, and she liked the special light pink straps Charlie Brown found for her to attach the mask to her face. She liked weird stuff like that.

She wore it diligently, every time she slept, naps included. We know grown men who are supposed to wear those things who struggle with them continually, throwing them off in the middle of the night. Not our girl - she loved hers! Each night we made all the right adjustments to ensure that the mask would fit tightly, as requested.

Next, we'd make sure that the mattress was propped up at the right angle, which helped with her breathing too. Then the pillows. We had to make sure they were in the correct order, hard one on the bottom, squishy one on top. Arm placement came next. She'd have us place the arm and shoulder that got sore while she slept on top of the perfectly sized stuffed animal (the big yellow and brown striped bee), in hopes of relieving pressure. She'd then usually want a drink of water, which meant taking the mask off to give it to her.

She was completely obsessed with concern her phone or iPad would run out of battery life overnight (although there was absolutely no chance of that happening). The minute she lost even one bar on the readout of battery life, she'd immediately have us plug the device in for recharging. So of course, at bedtime both of these items needed to be plugged in and placed next to her bed and checked over and over again to make sure the batteries were in fact charging.

She had two blankets that friends made for her. Bonnie from our church made one and delivered it to the hospital at the start of all the medical madness, unaware then that the blanket would be present and loved for the 22 surgeries to follow. The *"Bonnie Blanket"* was to be the first blanket to cover her followed by *"Kay's Blanket,"* the mostly red quilt she adored, quilted by our friend Kay complete with red fire trucks, dogs, red hearts and flowers.

Each night this choreography played out, and each night, after all had been accomplished to her satisfaction, the involuntary cozy-in-her-bed-before-sleep smile would appear, the before-sleep smile that began when she was a baby, the before-sleep sweet little grin that I can't recall a single night tucking her into bed without catching sight of.

Kisses and hugs goodnight were next. Kisses had to be on the forehead because that was the only part of her face exposed. Hugs given mostly by us because moving would require too much from her. Too much physically and too much readjusting. Some nights Curt would lay with her. She'd wrap her long narrow arm around his big solid one and hold his hand. They'd lay like that for a while, resting and caring and sharing, until she'd tell him it was time for him to go when she was ready to sleep. She never allowed any of us to sleep with her, including the dog, or her brother or sister, and this was something she was adamant about. It always made us chuckle when she'd tell us it was time to go.

Closing her door, we'd close our eyes too and offer up a silent prayer, then collapse on the sofa upstairs to wait for that first inevitably misspelled text of the night, *"sorry to brother you, i need your help pleasle."*

35

I thought of her today when.....

I THOUGHT OF her today when…

I woke up to the first snowfall of the season.

The first snowfall of the season is significant for our family and has been for the past thirty years because that's the day the candy tree blooms.

Legend of the Candy Tree dates back to when Jessie was a toddler. Some believe that my parents, waking up to the first snowfall of the season, discovered small wrapped candy bars blooming from the lowest branches of a tree outside their house. Others actually believe that my parents placed those candy bars on the tree with little wire hooks. Nevertheless, the candy tree bloomed in my parent's backyard (one way or another) the first snowfall of every year for twenty-seven years.

Predictably, when the kids were little, they loved the magic of the candy tree. They loved the experience of trudging through the snow all bundled up to pick the candy, and they loved sitting around the kitchen table drinking hot chocolate once the candy had been harvested.

Unpredictably, as the kids got older, they continued to love that candy tree. When they were in their teens, and their grandfather told them he thought the tree was done blooming, they begged him to keep it going. They told him how sad they'd be if the candy tree ceased to bloom and how sad so many of their cousins and friends would also be. Because of this, the candy tree has never, in all the years since its inception, missed a year of blooming.

Miraculously, when Curt and I became grandparents, the tree began to bloom at our house instead of Great Pop's, who says that's just what candy trees do - they bloom for new grandparents who really believe.

This year, the fourth year the tree has blossomed at our house, while Curt and I were outside checking on the blooms, all I could think of was how much fun the candy tree had been for my sweet girl every winter of her too short life. I pictured her small and excited in my dad's arms pulling candy from the tree; I pictured her the year she used a tiny walker, before she could actually walk on her own; trudging through the snow, determined to get to the tree on her own, I pictured Jason pulling down branches for her so she'd be able to reach; I pictured her finally able to walk and pull candy off the tree by herself; and I pictured her as she grew and began to help the smaller family friends and neighborhood kids we invited to fill their bags with candy. I pictured her the last year of her life telling her one-year-old nephew the Legend of the Candy Tree and just how it worked. For her especially, the magic of the candy tree never grew old.

I was never quite sure if she knew the truth about the candy tree. My dad had always been careful to hang the candy from the tree when she wasn't around, and he always made a big deal of how surprised and excited he was when it bloomed. We, of course, followed suit, stopping mid-sentence when we'd begin to say things in front of her about snow falling and candy purchases. We too spoke of how crazy it was that the tree always bloomed overnight or during the day when all the kids were at school. Other kids sometimes mentioned the wire hooks hanging from their candy, but she never did.

The day of this year's candy tree I remembered she'd written a story about the candy tree when she was in the fifth grade. I knew I had a copy of the story and could picture the spiral bound book's laminate cover. The paper was beige, the illustrations were drawn with thick black marker. The tree she drew filled up most of the page, and under the tree were stick figure children, each with an arm raised to the tree.

It was time to pull out the enormous blue treasure bin from the basement and find that book.

Rummaging through years and years of memories, forcing myself to push past letters and cards and report cards and art projects and photographs, somewhere in the middle of the bin, I found it, just as I'd remembered, The Candy Tree book, each page complete with a stick figure illustration, and a sentence or two written in her extra large, extra wobbly handwriting telling the story of the candy tree.

Reading her book confirmed most of my memories of how she felt about the candy tree. Page one told of how exciting the first snow of the season was for her and her brother and sister, and page two talked of the reason why. Pages three and four were about all the kids parading through the yard behind Pop, their fearless leader, singing songs on their way to the tree. Page five talked about sitting in the warm house after the candy had been pulled from the tree, but page six is where the shocker was, the shocker that I didn't remember. The caption under the illustration on page six reads, *"My Pop puts candy on the tree when it snows."*

So she knew.............That sweet girl knew the truth but let us carry on our little charade year after year —heck, she even helped to perpetuate it!

Two things are likely: the first was that it didn't matter to her how the candy got on the tree, and the second was that our feelings would be hurt if she spoiled the secret, so she didn't. Because that's just the kind of girl she was.

36

I thought of her today....

BECAUSE IT IS MAY 8th again.

The day she died (only four years later).

I've completed my annual litany of remembering each day (in infinite detail) of the week she died.

I remember her today and will continue to remember her every day.

My dad says it best when he talks about missing my mom. He states that the date on the calendar doesn't make his missing any greater or any less; he misses her everyday.

This year after remembering my girl and the week she died, I took the time to remember more; not more about those complicated days, but more about the days (turned years) since.

The days have been good.

I love and am loved by my husband more than ever.

I have, hands down, the best dad in the world who spends time with me and laughs with me and tells me he loves me every day.

I marvel at my children who as adults are wise and kind.

My friends are people I both adore and am in awe.

And my grandchildren know me well.

Today I affirm the healing.

It's May 8th again, the day I wish wasn't - but is.

37

Two Years After

I WORK OUT at the recreation center near our house. It's the same recreation center I used to take my daughter to swim the last couple summers of her life. I don't go into the locker room anymore; I don't like the memories that room holds for me. Instead, I change my clothes and shower at home.

But today I had to use the bathroom, which meant I had to go into the locker room, and just like every time I've walked into that dated room since she died, I walk right smack into a vision of her, a vision so clear it's like she hasn't been gone these last two years. She's sitting, hunched over like always, on the edge of the wooden bench in front of the faded yellow lockers. Her wet dark hair is plastered to the side of her face, and the beach towel with her name embroidered on it in big red letters is draped over her shoulders. Water drips off of her onto the mosaic tile floor as she waits for me to dry her.

I instinctively walk towards her, then force myself past the bench I know is empty and head for the privacy of the bathroom stall where I plan to slam the door on the uninvited memories that chase me down. The flimsy metal door is no match for memories. They have the ability to slip through the cracks of the pea green stall as well as the audacity to slide beneath the door that is both shut and locked.

It gets pretty crowded in that stall as each memory vies for attention. The one that fights its way to the top of the pile today is the one that reminds me of the protective, protective, sometimes defensive way I loved my girl, and the hurt loving her like that sometimes brought.

The memory that stalks me in the stall is the memory about the teenage lifeguards and the way they stared. Each morning the tanned and able-bodied teens stood together in their bathing suits leaning on the railing near the pool office. These kids were younger than my girl, and nowhere near as wise. Each day they'd watch us emerge, squinting and unsteady from the strangely comforting florescent light of the locker room, into the bright sunlight that surrounded the pool. Their stares unnerved me and had me acting like an insecure teenager myself. After my first few attempts of offering a good morning or a friendly smile had been met with rude stares and less than eager responses, I did my best to ignore the teens.

I so disliked the way they watched me hold my girl's arm in a vise grip (for fear that she'd fall on the hard concrete around the pool), while I juggled our big pool bag and a couple little lounge chairs over my shoulder as we made our way down to the shallow end of the pool (the side of the pool that made getting in and out of the water less awkward) where we sat with all the toddlers and their mothers.

I so disliked the way that I pretended that everything was fine and that the task at hand wasn't hard or humiliating or unnatural in anyway.

I have no trouble recalling the annoying fact that the lifeguards just stared at us. They never talked to us, never offered to help, never smiled. I try to be generous and believe they weren't sure what to do, but my generosity ran thin when what they chose to do, was nothing. Nothing that is, but watch us.

Because I was her mother and because I wanted to protect her, I didn't make the fuss I wanted to. I wanted to rip the fancy sunglasses from the faces of the lifeguards, and I wanted to shove each and every one of their tan little bodies right into the pool. The great satisfaction I would have experienced by letting them know how rude and ignorant they were acting would come in a distant second to the satisfaction that I would have derived from telling them that they were missing out on knowing a truly incredible girl.

Instead, I ignored them and hoped she didn't notice their stares. Instead, I kept her occupied by talking to her and joking with her and keeping her focused on finding us a place to sit. Instead, I carried on like everything was just the way we had planned.

She never knew they stared. She never knew the way they watched her as she slapped the water with her unsophisticated freestyle stroke. She never noticed how they stood by as we sometimes struggled to get her heavy legs out of the pool. She never knew I protected her; there was no reason for her to know.

Protecting her was my job. It was a job made just for me, and it was a job I was good at it. The hours were long, the days were full, the workplace stress sometimes tore my heart apart. But despite it all, I loved my job— and then my job was over.

There is more time in my day now for reflection when those workplace wounds come around to ambush me. There is more time to examine the hurt and understand it. Sometimes I think it was easier when I was busy doing instead of thinking.

So today, when the uncomfortable pool memory forced its way into the little bathroom stall with me, I saw it and felt it differently than I had in the past. I saw it with less fear and felt it with less indignation. I was able to look at it with compassion and wonder why I didn't ask for help. There is not a doubt in my mind that my girl would have welcomed the help, and there is not a doubt in my mind that it was my pride that kept me from asking.

It was time to patch the wound. It was time to forgive those snotty lifeguards (who maybe were more unsure of themselves than snotty) and time for me to forgive myself too. It was time to let go of this memory; it was time to move on.

Stepping from the bathroom stall, I expected to see her again on my way out of the locker room. I thought she'd still be sitting sopping wet on the bench where I left her, but she wasn't.

I caught a glimpse of her over by the mirror. She was dressed, her hair was dry and pretty and pulled back into a bright elastic headband - the kind she loved to wear. She looked back to me; she smiled, and then she waved, and she walked out the door.

38

Three Years After

THIS YEAR THE Christmas season stings less than it has the last three. I'm reluctant to admit that I'm growing used to life without her now, and have become acutely aware that wishing she were healthy and wishing she were here does not make it so. Therefore————I adapt, because I'm human and that's what we humans do; we adapt, even in the most heartbreaking of situations.

This year when I shopped and came across something she'd like, I'd hold on to it for a second, and say out loud, "This is for you." Then I'd picture how thrilled she'd be with the oversized athletic hoody that dangled from the hanger in my hand, or imagine how she'd dig through the gigantic bag of fruity-smelling lip balm on display, and joyfully over-apply each and every one of them. Satisfied with those happy images of her in my mind, I'd place the items back on the shelves and walk away with a real sense of delight. Fake-giving was fun, and it reminded me how sweet and happy and kind and simple and special she was. Fake-giving is something I plan to keep doing.

The Friday before Christmas this year, things were going right. My last minute search for pajamas, the gift that each member of our family knows they'll be getting from me on Christmas Eve, went smoother than expected. Target had just what I needed: four pairs long enough for the men in the family, two pairs small enough for the slim bodies of our grandchildren, one pair cozy sufficient for my liking, another pair slouchy enough to accommodate Jessie's adorable baby belly, where grand-baby number three remains for a few months more, and one long, red, zip-up-the-front-footy pair I chose to fake-give the daughter who spends Christmas with us, only in our hearts. I walked to my car that unseasonably warm winter day with a bit of a swagger; my Christmas shopping was done.

Walking through the Target parking lot, past the ridiculous number of dedicated accessible parking spaces that even I can say with certainty would never be filled at the same time unless there was a convention for people with disabilities taking place at Target, I noticed a woman unfolding and uprighting a wheelchair she'd obviously just removed from the rear of her big grey van. As she went through the familiar motions of straightening the seat cushion and lowering the footrests of the wheelchair, my eyes wandered to the passenger seat of the van where a young woman contentedly sat with a grin on her face, occupied with something she held on her lap. She looked to be around twenty years old and was waiting for her chariot to be readied.

My first inclination was to stop and talk with the woman who was preparing the wheelchair as she came around the of side the van because that's what I do when I see people with disabilities and their caretakers; I stop to talk with them; I can't help myself. My second inclination was to keep going.— I questioned my need to stop. Was I stopping because somehow stopping would make me feel better? Do the people I stop to chat with even want to talk or listen to what I have to say? And, what exactly was it that I was going to say if I did stop? I convinced myself this time, one of the few times ever, to just keep walking.

I found my little car, which is large enough for just two adults, and easily tossed my small bag of gifts into the trunk, acutely aware of how much my life has changed over the last three and a half years. I turned on the radio and headed out of the parking lot. When I approached the accessible spaces, I looked toward the big grey van just in time to see the lady who had successfully assembled the wheelchair begin to lift the younger woman from the passenger seat. She cradled her body carefully, the way a young mother carries her sleeping child, one arm placed under the child's head and neck, the other providing support under bent knees. The difference was this mother wasn't young, and the daughter wasn't young or sleeping either.

My first inclination was to pull into the parking space right next to them, and that's what I did. I had no idea what was going to happen next.

I opened my car door and stepped out as the young woman was being expertly placed into the seat of her chair.

"Hi!...... Is this your daughter?" Somehow, words formed on their own and tumbled out of my mouth.

"It is. This is Leila, and I'm Helen."

"Hi Helen, my name is Shelley." The words, inadequate as they were, kept coming, "I had a daughter that I used to help in and out of cars like you're doing."

Helen reached forward with both of her arms and wrapped me up in a warm and tender embrace. Helen's hug was the kind of hug your mom gives you when you hurt. Helen's embrace made me want to cozy in and cry. Helen's hug is a hug I will never forget.

"Is your daughter gone?" she whispered into my ear.

All I could manage was a shake of my head onto her shoulder.

I kneeled down to talk with Leila. I asked her if she was out Christmas shopping with her mother. Leila was non-verbal. She pointed to something in the car. Her mom knew just what she wanted and handed it to Leila. It was a stuffed animal that I think was a seal or an otter. Helen said that it was Leila's favorite, and that it had been given to her when she was a few days old; she said it went everywhere with them.

Helen and I spoke quietly together for a minute or two before she told her daughter that mine was in heaven, and that I missed her very much, and then she gave me another one of those enveloping hugs that I just wanted to rest in.

Wiping away tears, I told Leila that I thought her mom was terrific, and then looking into Helen's eyes I told her that my stopping was almost involuntary. I told her that I thought I stopped because I wanted her to know that I saw her and that I wanted her to know that I understand a little of what she does every day —and that I know how emotionally and physically tiring being a mom of an adult child with disability can be, and that I know how extraordinarily beautiful it can be too. I told her that I supposed I stopped also because I wanted to tell someone who would understand how much I miss being a mom of an adult child with a disability.

There were volumes more to say, but it was time to go. I wished Leila a very merry Christmas and hoped that she had a great day shopping with her mom.

Helen told me how glad she was that I had stopped, that it meant the world to her, and that she would never, ever forget me.

I got back into my little car, so grateful for the empathy that Helen and I had shared, and so grateful for the perfect timing it took for that to occur. Then I began to wonder what Helen was thinking as she pushed her daughter toward the store. Was she wondering, as I was, what it would be like to walk in the shoes of the other? Did her thoughts feel as unthinkable or at least as unsayable as mine? Was she imagining the daily struggle of life if her daughter weren't here, at the same time I was imagining the daily struggle of life if my daughter still were?

We adapt we humans, that's what we do, even in the most heartbreaking of situations.

Helen and I are no exception.

39

I thought of her today when...

I STAYED IN the shower long after the last of the shampoo had been washed from my hair. It was a cold morning, and I wasn't in a big hurry to leave the cozy, warm space I stood in. I stood there with nothing to do but let the warm water rush over me. I stood there and remembered, which is what I do a lot when there is nothing to do.

She used to like to write her name on the steamy glass of the shower. I pictured her long finger forming those oversized and crooked letters. I pictured the way she liked to dot the "i" in her name with a giant, five-pointed star.

I reached out my finger, and I drew her name on the shower door.

It made me smile to see it there.

Until the letters started to run, pieces of them disappearing as drops of water disfigured and pulled them down the length of the shower door.

I wiped her name away, which was worse than watching the letters harshly distort, so I quickly wrote it again toward the top of the door, a place where it would be safe from destructive drops of water.

I watched and remembered how much she loved her name. I watched and remembered how much I loved her name. I watched as her name disappeared,— slowly this time as the steam fought for its place at the top of the shower door.

This time watching the letters disappear wasn't as hard. This time they didn't become gnarled and mangled. This time they just faded away — a little at a time. The beauty was that their outline remained. When I looked hard enough, I saw where they once stood.

I shut off the water and got out of the shower. The water had warmed me and the knowledge that I can find her - that she's with me still, if I look close enough - warmed me even more. Her outline remains, and I take pleasure in finding it.

I see where she once stood, and I welcome the memory.

40

Four Years Later

I'VE READ ACCOUNTS of tornado and earthquake victims who comb through the debris of their destroyed homes in search of salvageable items. They speak with tender joy of finding personal items whole and intact. They speak of a comfort felt from finding and holding an item they'd presumed lost and gone forever. They speak of the emerging sense of hope and thankfulness that is reignited upon discovery of the item.

After she died, I combed through my own debris in search of salvageable items. I found one. It wasn't broken or gone. And it was, in fact, whole and intact. The item I found gives me an intensely tender sense of joy. The tangible item I was led to pull from my debris is an item uniquely hers. It is an item that reminds me, distinctively and without a doubt, who she was and how she lived. Like the other successful debris searchers I've read about, I am thankful for both the comfort that the item brings me and the continued sense of hope that it ignites in me, plus I just like having it with me - it's my secret weapon against Sad.

The item I found amid my debris was her name. And the

discovery so extraordinary, is that saying her name, or even thinking her name, fills me somehow with a profound completeness, that like a slow deep inhale has the ability to reach the empty far corners of my soul, and like a long slow exhale leaves the corners of my mouth turned slightly (almost imperceptibly) up in to a grin. Saying her name, or even thinking her name, reminds me all at once of everything she was, and everything we were together. Saying her name or even thinking her name is good.

Her name was Hallie.

Hallie Elizabeth.

Twenty-seven years ago when I carried her in my belly the name came to mind. I loved the name then because it was unique. I've loved the name every day since because the name was hers.

Simply stating that she too was fond of her name would be an understatement. Her name was one of those things in her life that made her happy, one of the things she grabbed onto and delighted in, like firetrucks and helicopters. She was proud of her name, maybe for the same reason I was, because the name was hers.

She never hesitated to point out to an individual the egregious error of their ways when they mistakenly pronounced her name Hailey instead of Hallie. The number of doctors and nurses she corrected on this were too many to count (and often times had me wondering if these were the people I should be trusting with my girl's life, when they didn't even know the basic rules of the English language). It was important to her (and to me) that she be called by the correct name, "*My name is Hallie,"* she'd tell them, *"H- A- double L- I- E."*

When she signed her name, she signed it with a flourish. Instead of the usual dot over the "i" that most of us use, she thought it vital and very glamorous to take the time to draw a rather sizable misshapen star over the second to last letter of her name. Sometimes she'd draw atop that very same letter an oversized circle that without fail had to be colored in with either the pen she was using (when she was in a hurry), or preferably a pen of a different color when she had the time.

It wasn't just her first name she was proud of either. Her middle name, or more accurately, her middle initial was crucial to her. School papers usually included her first name, last name, and middle initial; the many cards and letters she signed over the years, even to us, were usually signed, Hallie E.

She'd sit by my side in doctor's offices double checking my work as I filled out forms for her. I'd get the thumbs up, or in her case, the *"double thumbs up"*, the highest honor she bestowed (and did so by placing both her thumbs to either side of her cheeks) only when she was confident that her middle initial had been clearly included on all documents that required her name.

Hallie: it's a name that suited her well. Hallie, to me at least, sounds cute and happy. And against all the odds, our girl was just that - so cute and so happy.

Hallie: it's a simple name, a name that, like our girl, is without pretense. The name Hallie seems to say what our girl would have liked to say to everyone she met, *"Here I am, I've nothing to hide —I want to get to know you because I really want you to know me."*

Hallie: it's a young sounding name, and the perfect name for our sweet girl who will forever remain young.

We called her Hal. I still call her Hal. I call her Hal when I think about her, when I talk with family and friends about her and occasionally when I just talk directly to her and tell her how much I miss her.

Accounts vary on just what it is that people do with treasure uncovered. Some, afraid of loss or future destruction, hide their items away in fireproof boxes and tell of the comfort they find in the certainty that their items are safe. Some display their items in a place of honor for all to see and speak of the comfort that comes from the remembering and the retelling of their story. Others, rely on the use of their items, like a favorite set of candlesticks, or a blanket found beneath the rubble. They use their items every day and take joy in their use. Each of these people speaks of holding onto their items because they are the link to what once was, the peace for what now is, and a hope for what is to come.

I have no real chance I'll lose the item I've pulled from my debris. There is no real chance that her name will be damaged or broken, yet I protect it. I'm fairly certain that I use her name every day. Some days I proudly display it, and some days I hold it close to my chest where I know it will be safe.

I'm careful with her name.

Her name holds weight and has value.

I don't want to dilute it.

I don't use it recklessly.

I don't share it with just anyone.

I share her name with people who take the time to understand. I share her name carefully and cautiously with those who didn't have the chance to know her, but wish they did. I share her name with those who knew her, with those who loved her, and with those who remember her. I share her name with people who take the time to listen.

Today, I share her name with you.